△

# 50 YEARS OF
# GLASTONBURY

THIS IS A CARLTON BOOK

Published by Carlton Books Ltd
20 Mortimer Street
London W1T 3JW

ISBN 978-1-78739-264-9

Editorial Director: Roland Hall
Editorial Assistant: Georgia Goodall
Design: Russell Knowles
Production: Yael Steinitz
Picture Research: Steve Behan

A CIP catalogue for this book is available from the British Library

10 9 8 7 6 5 4 3 2 1

Printed in Dubai

# 50 YEARS OF
# GLASTONBURY

## MUSIC AND MUD AT THE ULTIMATE FESTIVAL

FOREWORD
SIR RAY DAVIES

INTRODUCTION
TOM RAVENSCROFT

MALCOLM
CROFT

CARLTON
BOOKS

# CONTENTS

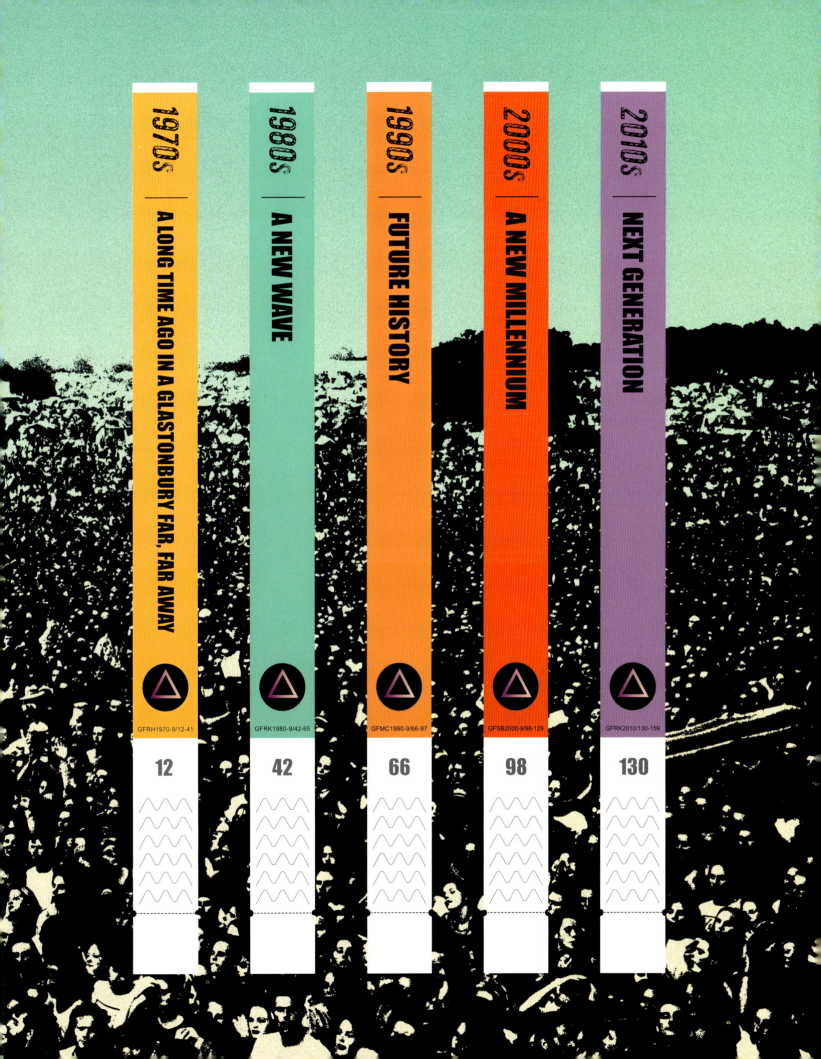

1970s | A LONG TIME AGO IN A GLASTONBURY FAR, FAR AWAY

GFRH1970-9/12-41

12

1980s | A NEW WAVE

GFRK1980-9/42-65

42

1990s | FUTURE HISTORY

GFMC1990-9/66-97

66

2000s | A NEW MILLENNIUM

GFSB2000-9/98-129

98

2010s | NEXT GENERATION

GFRK2010/130-159

130

# FOREWORD

*I* didn't feel like playing. Even the thought of picking up my guitar and walking on to a stage filled me with dread. On top of which the journey to the West Country would be jammed with traffic all on the way to Glastonbury. It was the day after Michael Jackson died and it seemed inappropriate to play a gig of any description.

I'd played the Acoustic Tent before with my two-man show and enjoyed it. I'd played the Pyramid Stage years earlier with my band the Kinks and loved it. But today it just didn't seem right.

Eventually our Toyota Previa van reached the sprawling site and we were ushered through to the backstage area by the super-efficient security guards. I sat alone while I waited for my road manager to give me the 15 minute call. I didn't even bother to get changed into my regular stage gear and I kept my muddy wellies on.

My name was announced and I walked on. I considered standing in a moment's silence… and instead of going into my first song I stood and stared at the crowd like I was a prize fighter eyeballing my opponent before the fight. Somehow the audience picked up on my mood and started to cheer. The longer I stared the louder they cheered. It was almost a telepathic encounter as though the audience and I were having a conversation.

"I can't do it."

"Oh yes you can. You know you can."

The tent started to fill up past its capacity as though word had got out that something special was happening. Through a gap in the folds of the tent I could see the sun peek through a dark cloud as it often does in Glastonbury. Being born on the summer solstice I knew intuitively a show would be alright to play after all.

I played my show in the Acoustic Tent and even the field beyond seemed full of humanity and compassion and I thought… Glasto is not just a music festival… it is a mythical place full of good music and, more than anything else, it has more than any other festival: a sense that the place is full of healing properties.

And if that is not enough, Michael Eavis is always around to point you in the right direction.

*Sir Ray Davies, London, 20 December 2018.*

As young teens we'd peer excitedly out of the car window as the world slowly got hillier and greener, eagerly anticipating our first glimpse of a stripy marquee below in the valley, or the start of the processions of crusties worming their way down miles of slim country roads in search of an entrance. In its earlier, slightly wilder days, Glastonbury Festival could be quite an intimidating place. Long before everyone started making an effort to look nice and bringing their own chairs, it was mostly people in army surplus gear, burning rubbish and listen to dub reggae or trance.

There wasn't a great deal of children around then – we'd get pointed at a lot and have our hair ruffled by strangers. However, it didn't take long for us to realize this was, in fact, a very safe and special place, a place where we could surprisingly be more ourselves than we'd ever been able to before. It's an inclusive community that pops up for a few days and promotes a far more fun and positive take on the world, and then suddenly disappears. It has since become a home from home.

The Glastonbury Festival has always been uniquely magical. The list of bands involved each year is a testament to how important it is for so many musicians to get to play there. Long ago I stopped circling band names and times on programmes and instead took to the method of wandering aimlessly until my feet hurt, and then planting myself. This has proven wholly successful. For wherever you end up, there is something to laugh at, something to learn, someone lovely to meet, something gorgeous to eat and something wonderful to listen to. I feel immensely lucky to have been to Glastonbury so many times and to have experienced so many wonderful things. It's a festival to be cherished and a festival to be partied hard at – until those famous cows come home.

*Tom Ravenscroft, London, December 2018*

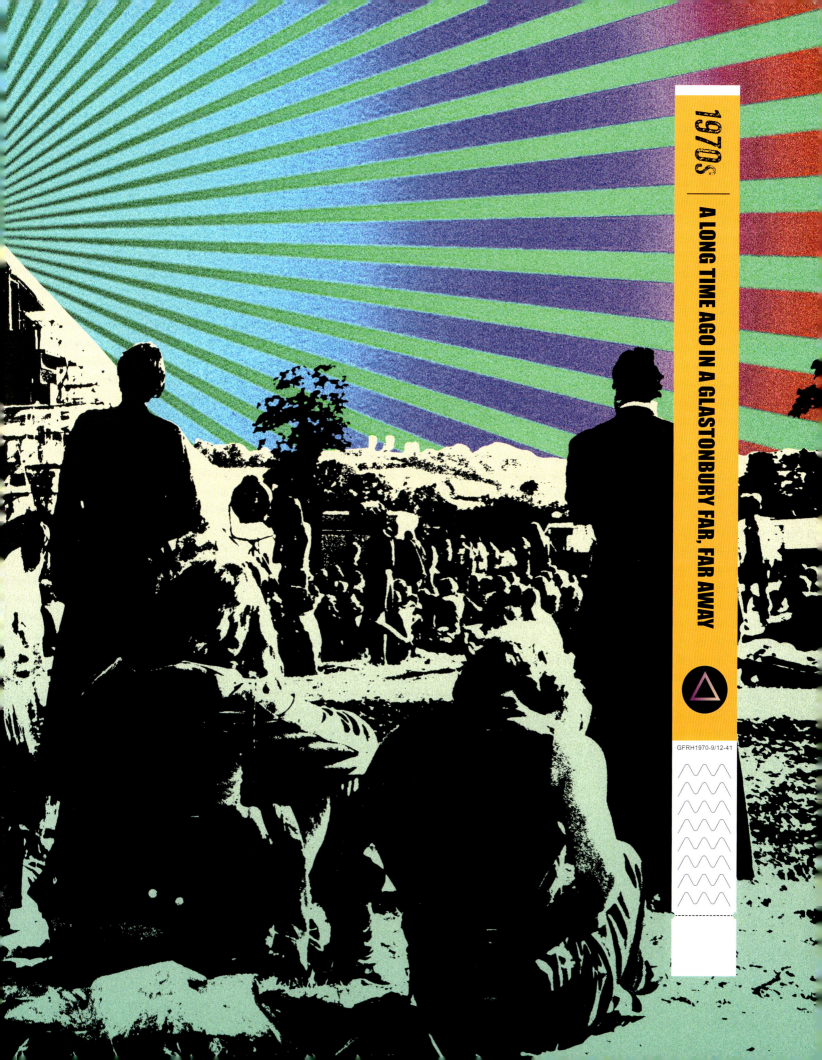

1970s

A LONG TIME AGO IN A GLASTONBURY FAR, FAR AWAY

GFRH1970-9/12-41

**1970s**

UP UNTIL 1970, MICHAEL EAVIS REGARDED HIS FAMILY AS "COW PEOPLE" – FARMERS WHO HAD NO GREATER AMBITION THAN TENDING TO THE NATURAL NEEDS OF WORTHY FARM, 150 ACRES OF LILTING FIELDS AND LAKES SET INSIDE THE ANCIENT LANDS OF SOMERSET, A LANDSCAPE RICH WITH LEGEND AND BEAUTY. FOR 150 YEARS AND SIX GENERATIONS, THE EAVIS CLAN LIVED THE SIMPLE LIFE, A GOOD LIFE, AT THEIR ANCESTRAL HOME. "I NEVER REALLY SAW MYSELF AS A FESTIVAL ORGANIZER," MICHAEL, THE NOW 83-YEAR-OLD PATRIACH, REVEALED. "I JUST SORT OF WADED INTO IT REALLY. I DIDN'T KNOW WHAT I WAS DOING."

Today, five decades later, Michael – he of legendary beard and bald pate – is the god-like figurehead of Glastonbury, and Worthy Farm is indeed worthy of hosting the largest greenfield and contemporary performing arts festival in the world. Or, as *Vice* magazine once nailed it: "the world's greatest five-day farmyard bender".

The festival is without question a beloved national treasure – an iconic annual "happening", revered for bringing together the biggest artists and most thrilling contemporary art attractions. However, this actually feels like an understatement when you consider the numbers involved in operating such a colossal event every year that it takes place. Glastonbury is, quite simply, the biggest show on earth. The festival now covers more than 1,500 acres, welcomes almost 200,000 punters every year, features more than one million square metres of camping space and pays more than 100,000 members of staff to keep everywhere safe and tidy. Thankfully, there are also more than 5,000 portable toilets to keep up with the incessant demand of so many revellers.

Michael Eavis, the founder and architect of all these shenanigans, still proudly identifies himself as a farmer. However, the truth is that, as of 2015, he was named by *Time* magazine as one of the most influential people on the planet. He didn't have time to bathe in the compliment: "I've got cows to sort out," he replied.

### BEFORE THE BEGINNING

The origins of the Glastonbury festival are as humble as its founders. "I always liked pop music," Michael told *Arty Farty* magazine. "When I was at school I was really keen on the Who, Elvis Presley and all that sort of thing. I was always keen on music; but when I went to the Bath Blues festival I got the idea for Glastonbury."

On 19 September 1970, Michael and his second wife Jean launched the Pilton Festival – or the Worthy Farm Pop Festival, as it was also known at the time. This was conceived as a "hippie happening" which, according to legend, Michael hit upon after he and Jean sneaked through a hedge to watch Led Zeppelin perform at the Shepton Mallet Blues Festival near Bath a few months earlier. "I fell in love," Michael told *IQ* magazine. "They had Led Zeppelin, Pink Floyd, all these west coast US bands." It was while in Bath that Michael met, and enjoyed, his first hippies – "real flower power types; they were splendid!"

The idea for the festival chimed so perfectly with Michael's Methodist "love and peace" upbringing that it inspired him to get on the phone and call bands. He concedes that at that point he didn't know what he would do with them if they actually said "yes", but he was willing to take the risk. "I called the venue in Bristol where we went to local concerts, told them I was looking for the Kinks, and they gave me their manager's number. So, I called him and he said they would do it for £500."

"I've been a huge risk-taker all my life," Michael told the *Metro* newspaper. I mean, 50 years of huge risks really and so far, touch wood, I haven't come unstuck."

The genesis of the Worthy Farm Pop Festival may have arisen from a spiritual awakening in Bath, but Eavis's desire to do something different was primarily driven, as always, by financial necessity. "The farm is such a dead loss we've got to look at other ways of making money," Michael told the *Scotland Herald*. "My father died when I was just 19 and the farm was on the verge of collapse. I took out a £5,000 loan to buy the land, and to turn it around involved a lot of hard work. We had 150 acres and 60 cows at the time," he explained to the *Mail Online*. At the time, Michael and Jean thought they were crazy even to consider putting on a festival. "It was a very radical thing to do, but it derived from the same trait that produced Methodism in the first place, where you challenge the status quo and the establishment," he recalled. "It's important to me even now."

Hoping that if he booked the bands, they would come, Michael set forth on an adventure of founding his own version of the Bath Blues Festival. Sadly, not all the bands he booked came. The Kinks, one of Michael's, and his cows' most beloved bands ("I play 'Lola' to the cows, right into the dairy, down a long pipe so the bass is absolutely fantastic."), didn't turn up, despite being advertised on the flyer along with "at least six other groups!" Wayne Fontana was also a no-show.

"The Kinks were going to play," Michael recalled, "but they pulled out because they quite rightly thought we were amateurs." As it transpired, the truth was that the *Melody Maker* ran a headline that read "Kinks to play mini-festival" – and the band didn't like the idea of playing anything "mini"... "I think they were a bit insulted by that," Michael said. "After all, they were at the top of the charts with 'Lola' at the time. All the posters still said it was the Kinks playing, though."

So, on 19 September 1970, the Worthy Farm Pop Festival opened its doors. Results were mixed, according to those who were there. Which wasn't many. "Not many people turned up," Michael remembered. The line-up wasn't that bad either, all things considered. Quintessence, Amazing Blondel, Keith Christmas, Duster Bennet, Sam Apple Pie, Stackridge, Steamhammer, Al Stewart and Planxty all appeared on the bill.

No question, the headline act not turning up was a disaster – but it was another turn of bad fortune that really put a dampener on the first festival. On 18 September 1970, the world awoke to the news that Jimi Hendrix had died of asphyxia in his sleep and moved on to another celestial plain. He was just 27. "Hendrix had agreed to play the event, but unfortunately he died the day after he made the promise," remembers Andrew Kerr, Glastonbury 1971's co-founder.

With Worthy Farm feeling not very worthy of a festival – only 1,500 people showed up (out of an anticipated 5,000), despite its tiny entrance fee of £1, including free milk! – and no one in a mood to party, the future of Glastonbury was looking muddied. Thankfully, Marc Bolan and his glittery-band T. Rex pitched up (en route to Butlins, Minehead, of all places) and put in an unforgettable performance that brightened everyone's day, in tandem with the appearance of the sunshine.

"Marc Bolan was on his way to play at Butlins and sneaked us in," Michael recalled to *New Musical Express*. "To this day, it remains one of the most memorable slots ever at the festival to me. He came in and did the ultimate rock 'n' roll gig. He was so professional; he wasn't put off by the fact we didn't know what we were doing, just dairy farmers having a bit of a party. Bolan played on and on and on as the sun was going down... all the hits, the full works, and it sounded fantastic."

Michael's recollection of T. Rex's headline-saving show is more favourable than his first impression of Marc Bolan.

"He was really grumpy when he arrived, and I was trying to be nice to him by brushing the leaves off his car, doing the whole jolly farmer thing. He wouldn't have any of it. "He said, 'Don't touch my car!' and I thought, 'Oh my God, we've got someone really grumpy and he hasn't even started yet!' It was my first ever confrontation with a rock star."

T. Rex got paid £500 for their headline performance, though not all at once. "I couldn't pay the band," Eavis remembered. "I told him,

'I can't pay you, but I'll give you £100 per month for five months.' He got paid, but he wasn't happy about it – the cows pretty much paid for T. Rex."

It may have been a short-term loss, but T. Rex's set gave Michael "the courage to carry on with the festival. It was so inspiring to me. It was a pivotal point to me ... a brilliant, brilliant set." The punters who came for the first Glastonbury almost agreed with him. Almost. "Very poor attendance, I think mainly due to bad advertising," said one. "Could have been a gas, great show, had it been better advertised." Michael was on to a winner, he just needed to do better next year: "I had the land and I had the farm, and I thought it was a wonderful idea," he exclaimed. "The incredible response I have had from the people that did come has wiped out the gloom of not managing to make a profit. I wouldn't say it was a disaster, but it hasn't been as good as I hoped." It would require a couple of hippies to persuade Michael to put on another festival. Thankfully, Arabella Churchill and Andrew Kerr arrived precisely at the right place at the right time...

## THE FIRST "GLASTONBURY FAYRE"

Shortly after the first Worthy Farm festival, Michael welcomed to his home two "hippie dreamers" in the distinguished forms of Andrew Kerr and Arabella Churchill, the grand-daughter of Winston Churchill. The duo were keen to meet the Methodist farmer who was brave enough to put on a music festival outside London. Inspired by the American Woodstock counterculture vibe of 1969, Kerr and Churchill were seeking a UK "happening" with honourable intentions and they thought Worthy Farm had all the right ingredients. "I was getting a bit fed up with the commercialism of the festivals like the Isle of Wight," recalled Kerr to *The Independent*. "I understood there was a bit of corruption going on. There seemed to be a need for a truly free festival. All the others had some profit motive behind them – some for worthy causes, some for greed, none for love."

As Michael Eavis recalls: "Andrew came to me in 1970 with ideas to run a free festival, and with the help of Arabella Churchill and others he raised the necessary funds," he told *The Independent*. "Kerr had a job on his hands trying to make the project happen," Michael recalled, "but Churchill and Kerr were in crusading mode, the eco-warriors of their day."

According to Michael, it was Kerr's and Churchill's energy and passion that turned his dream of a successful festival at Worthy Farm into a reality, even if both Churchill and Kerr sidelined Michael for the first outing in order to make this happen. "Andrew Kerr brought a new green conviction to the farm," recalled Michael, "raising environmental and ecological concerns to a national level of debate for the very first time. The Glastonbury we know now owes so much to his vision."

Churchill, who died in 2008, received similar praise from Michael in her published obituary. "Arabella was one of the key figures in the Glastonbury Festival. Involved with the organization since the 'Glastonbury Fayre' of 1971, for the next 37 years she was a most valuable member of the team, and from 1981 responsible for programming and running the theatre and circus fields at the festival."

For the 1971 event, Churchill and Kerr outlined to Michael their major plans for the "Glastonbury Fayre", including dousing the land for ley lines upon which to place the stage and creating an area where alien spaceships could land, should they be whizzing past and wishing to stop off at a festival.

The duo lived at Worthy Farm for some time, putting their heads together and concocting an even greater event than even Michael could have believed possible. "It just turned me on, the whole thing," he told the *New York Times*. Churchill quipped in 2007: "When you think that it's run by old duffers like me and Michael, the fact that so many people want to come to Glastonbury is very flattering... I don't think I've let the family down at all, have I?"

Financial backing for the 1971 event came from Churchill. Becoming "funded by rich upper-crust hippies" amused Michael Eavis no end. Arabella Churchill was only 21 years old at the time and she came from rich stock; at one point she was even considered to be a potential future wife for Prince Charles. However, Arabella disliked her aristocratic origins and strongly resisted any pressure to become royalty. "I felt I wanted to be a hippie, I felt I was left-wing, I didn't feel like the rest of my family," Churchill recalled of the time. "My family, we are all Churchills, but some of us are more Churchillian than others. I like to think I am very Churchillian," she said, "... in the sense that I am adventurous, independent and tough". As Michael told *The Independent*: "Arabella had an uncompromising compassion for humanity, a great sense of morality and social responsibility and a willingness to work tirelessly to achieve a result." The money put up by Churchill's pals notionally meant that Michael did not have to stress too much about losing money. As it happened, he ended up £1,500 out of pocket, but nonetheless declared: "The event was a huge success – the best investment I've ever made."

Costing somewhere in the region of £40,000, the 1971 Glastonbury Free Festival proved a hit with 8,500 revellers – mainly "upper-crust hippies", who turned on, tuned in and dropped out. Entrance was free, but in a bid to maximize profits festival revellers were encouraged to buy milk from Michael during their stay.

In the early Seventies, commercial fatigue had set in among some music fans – and particularly ageing hippies such as Andrew Kerr – who were weary of just how corporate and money-driven pop and rock festivals such as the Isle of Wight Festival had become. There were a number of events that now took place annually across the country, the result of contemporary teenagers' insatiable desire for rock 'n' roll. Promoters and events companies were quick to realize that these young consumers also had plenty of disposable cash and devised as many ways as possible to make them part with it.

The new Glastonbury festival – with its hippie roots and medieval tradition of fusing music, dance, poetry, theatre and lights – presented a refreshing change of scene. With a new date in the calendar, summer solstice – brought forward from the first festival's September 1970 slot – the fayre positioned itself as a true one-of-a-kind happening, which drew the attention of hippies, budding ecologists and young music fans alike.

The leaflet promoting the 1971 festival, written by Andrew Kerr, set out the free-spirited ambitions of the trio of organizers: "Man is fast ruining his environment. He is suffering from the effects of pollution; from the neurosis brought about by a basically urban industrial society; from the lack of spirituality in his life. The aims of Glastonbury are, therefore: the conservation of our natural resources, a respect for nature and life and a spiritual awakening."

Over the five-day event, 35 acts played in a field on Worthy Farm. Popular acts the Grateful Dead, the Who and Pink Floyd were asked by promoter friends of Michael's to add a little international clout to the proceedings, but they couldn't make it. Instead, Hawkwind returned (they had played in 1970), alongside Steve Winwood's pop group, Traffic. In addition to these big-name acts, Joan Baez, Fairport Convention and Arthur Brown put in appearances on the main – in fact, the only – stage. Kerr introduced each band with a short environmentally friendly speech, enlightening the music-loving fans that the festival stood for a lot more than just music.

The surprise guest of the 1971 fayre was David Bowie. He performed a seven-song set, at dawn, on 23 June, a mere week after his first ever appearance on *Top of the Pops*. "The fans came for Bowie," Eavis recalled. Bowie played a solo performance, supported by just guitar and keyboards, of the songs "Oh! You Pretty Things", "Kooks", "Changes", "Amsterdam", "The Supermen", "Memory of a Free Festival" and "Song For Bob Dylan". His stellar set revealed his obvious ascension to the laps of the gods in the process. As Bowie himself remembered, sort of: "It was 1971 and I was bottom of the bill… I was originally scheduled to go on at around midnight but things got so delayed that I didn't make it on stage until around five in the morning. So, what better than to spend the intervening hours ensconced in the farmhouse, along with a crew of latter-day hippies, and all kinds of mushrooms. By the time I was due to perform I was flying and could hardly see my electric keyboard or my guitar." When Bowie performed again in 2000, he wore a replica of the same coat and trousers that he had worn on stage in 1971, much to Michael Eavis's great delight.

Away from the live stage, Glastonbury's adjacent fields were sparsely populated by an eclectic mix of 12,500 people – head-bangers, tribal drummers, exotic religionists, nude exhibitionists, mystics and wizards, film superstars (Julie Christie) and even supermodels – "Jean Shrimpton made lentils," Michael remembered. One thing connected them all, if not Michael Eavis. "Everybody was high. We were all high, man! Everybody!," observed Quintessence singer Phil Shiva Jones from Nicolas Roeg's 1972 documentary of the festival, *Glastonbury Fayre*.

While the punters were having a good time, Michael was upset by the effects of the festival on his cattle, as well as Kerr's and Churchill's attitudes to the people of Pilton, the local village, and Michael's neighbours. "There was a lot of LSD about, and people were freaking out, wandering into the village wearing only a top hat," Michael recalled. Even the now-veteran news reporter, John Craven, turned up for a news report (in a suit and tie), and agreed with Michael's observations: "… aspects such as the free love-making, the fertility rites, the naked dancing and most of all, the drug-taking. There had been pot and acid, that's cannabis and LSD, but there have only been two arrests and police said they were quite surprised and pleased about the way the festival had gone on," he told the squares watching at home.

In 1971, the name of Michael Eavis's festival was changed from Worthy Farm Pop Festival to Glastonbury Fayre. This happened when Arabella Churchill and Andrew Kerr introduced Michael to an author named John Michell, who had just written a book entitled *The View over Atlantis*. In the book, Michell wrote that, due to its legendary location and possible connection to King Arthur, Avalon and Joseph of Arimathea, Glastonbury was the New Jerusalem. "John Michell wanted me to change the name of the festival," recalled Michael. "Glastonbury had always been a centre for us anyway in Pilton: it's only six miles away, so we naturally gravitated there. So, mentally and emotionally it was all about Glastonbury." Indeed, for a thousand years, Glastonbury Abbey was considered "the most spectacular abbey in all Christendom," as Jon Cousins, the town's former mayor, exclaimed. "It was so important that in Italy they called it *Roma Secunda* – the Second Rome."

Back in Pilton, Glastonbury Festival 1971 was deemed a success due to two key factors later ascribed by Michael: "great weather and not too many people turned up". Andrew Kerr added: "People had heard about it, and it was all word of mouth. We had no idea who was going to turn up, it may have been nobody, we didn't know. There was just no way to tell. Then the Press started to get interested. The local Press were obviously quite interested, and the villagers. Some of them were rather sceptical, and some were pleased. It's quite a thing to invade a quiet Somerset village, when a whole load of hippies come out of the cities." Kerr concluded: "1971 – that was the first large Glastonbury Festival."

It would be seven years before Glastonbury was played again.

## SEVEN YEARS LATER

Left reeling by the shock, awe – and sheer mess – that the 1971 event inflicted upon the fields of Worthy Farm, Michael Eavis was in no rush to put the festival on again. Indeed, even the next event – which took place in 1978 – was an unplanned, impromptu gathering, rather than a proper festival. Michael required much persuasion to go again. "After 1971, Michael didn't have a festival for quite a long time. I returned in 1978 when there was a spontaneous free festival there," Andrew Kerr remembered.

As such, 1978 became known as the "impromptu" Glastonbury festival. This happened with the arrival of travellers leaving the summer solstice at Stonehenge who were led to believe that another festival was taking place down the road from Glastonbury – though the police thwarted their plans. After some persuading, Michael agreed that a mini-festival could be staged. As Andrew Kerr recalled in 2014: "All the people from Stonehenge had been chucked off by police. As Michael was driving back to Glastonbury, there was this convoy of vans and Michael was stopped by this policeman who was escorting the vans and the conversation went like this:

Michael: 'Where are you going with this lot?'

Police: 'We're going down your farm.'

Michael: 'You can't do that, we haven't got any facilities.'

Police: 'You still haven't got that van taxed and insured have you?'

Michael: 'OK, just for the night.'

That's how the 1978 festival happened," Kerr remembered.

In the convoy of vans from Stonehenge were more than 500 hippies looking to continue digging their summer solstice vibes. Unprepared, Michael allowed the revellers to pitch up, even helping out on his tractor when the hippies' mode of transport got stuck in the mud. Hawkwind, Sphinx and "a band from East Anglia" – as well as a clown and mime or two – performed on what could only very generously be called a stage, powered by a cable running across a field to an electric meter in a caravan. According to Nik Turner, a performer in 1979, Kerr was seen running around saying, "This is better than '71".

Perhaps surprisingly, this impromptu gathering was indeed considered a success, giving Michael Eavis the confidence to try again the following year. It was a bold decision.

In spring 1979, Andrew Kerr, Arabella Churchill and Michael Eavis reconvened at Worthy Farm to discuss the third Glastonbury Fayre. They decided that a three-day event would generate a comfortable level of profit, in order to make all the stress and mess worthwhile. They agreed that they would charge an entrance fee of £5, in the hope that more than 10,000 people would come.

Churchill wanted to stage an event in honour of the UN Year of the Child, giving Michael the idea to link the festival with a good cause. Accordingly, Glastonbury Festival came to be associated with the CND movement (Campaign for Nuclear Disarmament) for the whole of the next decade.

Michael secured the services of ex-Genesis singer Peter Gabriel – who was currently enjoying a very successful solo career – with his old bandmate Phil Collins on drums. He raised the funds necessary to land such a star with a bank loan secured with the deeds of Worthy Farm as collateral. This was a huge risk that only a risk-taker such as Michael was willing to take. Accompanying Gabriel on the main stage were other acts such as Tim Blake, the Sensational Alex Harvey Band, Steve Hillage, Mother Gong, Nik Turner, Footsbarn Theatre, Sky and John Martyn. Alongside these hippie-folk acts, punk bands such as the Pop Group and Only Ones added a little more bite to the proceedings.

For Michael Eavis, the appearance of his personal hero John Martyn made the event worth it, with his set entering Michael's list of Top Five performances to date. "We had quite a stormy relationship really. But on that occasion, at that moment in time, he was perfect." Unfortunately, not even John Martyn's set could save the fortunes of the festival. It ended with a large financial loss, meaning that Glastonbury 1980 was vetoed until Michael, Churchill and Kerr could rethink their strategy.

As the new decade arrived, with its alternative outlook on life, fashion and drug-taking, Glastonbury returned in 1981. This time the festival boasted not only a proper management structure, but also a renewed sense of purpose, thanks largely to the birth of Michael's youngest daughter, Emily.

Below: Revellers at the first fayre take a match to Michael Eavis's cart, 1970.

"I went to the Bath Festival of Blues and Progressive Music in 1970 and I thought: 'This is for me!' There was an amazing display of talent – all the best bands in the world were there. It was a very powerful message."

Michael Eavis

Above: Fun for all the family: an infant plays amongst the hippie revelry, 1970.

Opposite above: Mr Tambourine Man: Quintessence's Shiva Shankar Jones, 1970.

Opposite below: An acoustic performer awaits their stage time, 1970.

Top: Michael Eavis in portrait mode, 1971.

Above: From Stonehenge and the summer solstice, the hippies' pilgrimage to the parties at Glastonbury, 1971.

Left: The Pyramid Stage makes a wondrous first impression at the second festival, 1971.

GO EASY !!!!!...

Previous pages: The hunt for fresh water continues, 1971.

Opposite: The first incarnation of Andrew Kerr and Bill Harkin's Pyramid Stage, 1971.

Below: A visitor kindly waters the flowers next to the Pyramid Stage, 1971.

## THE FIRST PYRAMID STAGE

The first iteration of the Pyramid Stage was conceived by Andrew Kerr and made its appearance at the festival in 1971. Today it is probably the defining symbol of the festival – a shining light of the farm's heritage, mythology, ambition and grandiosity. Once doubling as a cowshed and feed store for Michael's 400 cows during the winter months, the Pyramid Stage is now the focus for all the festival's biggest acts, and the performance zenith for all aspiring bands.

Arabella Churchill invested £4,000 in the "Psychic Pyramid" stage, as it was known, and Andrew Kerr chose the location. Kerr believed that the right spot was over a spring (which he had found by dousing), directly connected to the Stonehenge–Glastonbury ley line. With the timing of the festival occurring at Midsummer, it was important to Kerr that the event remained close to the pagan calendar – hence the bringing forward of the festival from September to June. "What we were trying to do was to stimulate the Earth's nervous system with joy, appreciation and happiness, so that our Mother planet would respond by breeding a happier,

more balanced race of men, animals and plants," Kerr stated. In 50 years, the stage hasn't shifted.

It probably comes as no surprise, then, that the design of the Pyramid Stage came to its creator, Bill Harkin, in a dream. "I had a dream about standing at the back of a stage and seeing two beams of light forming a pyramid and took that as a message," said theatre designer Harkin, having met Kerr during a chance meeting at Glastonbury Tor, one of the area's most popular and ancient spiritual hot-spots. Harkin's vision led him to replicate Cairo's Great Pyramid of Giza – scaled down to one-tenth of the size of the original. "A pyramid is a very powerful shape: the apex projects energy upwards while energy from the stars and sun are drawn down. The original Pyramid resembled a diamond transmitting pure vibrations into the night," recalled Harkin on his original design. Since 1971, the Pyramid Stage has had three different designs implemented in 1971, 1981 and 2000. Today's Pyramid is the largest of all, measuring 30 metres (90 feet) tall and constructed out of 4 kilometres (2.5 miles) of steel piping.

Opposite above: Campers set up shop, 1971.

Opposite below: No frills camping, as it all was back in 1971.

Below: Giving thanks to the sun at solstice, 1971.

Above left: A family festival since it began, 1971.

Above right: Glastonbury – full of golden wonder since '71.

Opposite above: A whole lot of hippies chanting and dancing, 1971.

Opposite below: Friends and families entertain themselves between acts, 1971.

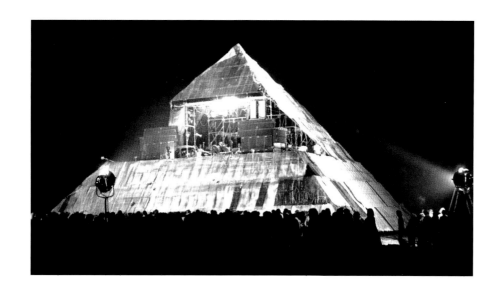

Above: The Pyramid takes centre stage at night, 1971.

Left: David Jones puts on his Bowie costume ahead of his now-famous '71 appearance.

Opposite: Revellers hold hands: a splendid view from the top of the Pyramid Stage, 1971.

"Don't get me wrong, I love the festival. That's why
it's so successful – because I love it so much. But
if you offered me a preference, I prefer the farm."
Michael Eavis

**Midsummer 21st—23rd June 1979**

3 DAYS GREEN £5

2 DAYS BLUE £4

1 DAY RED £3

INC____VAT

№ 01041          № 01041

TICKETS ARE SOLD SUBJECT TO THE FOLLOWING CONDITIONS.

1) The organisers reserve the right to refuse admission (ticket money paid may be refunded to anyone refused admission)

2) Tickets will not be exchanged or money refunded (except as above)

3) The organisers reserve the right to alter any announced billing of bands or other events.

4) The organisers reserve the right to make changes, if necessary due to unavoidable circumstances, to any of the Fayre arrangements.

Above: You are cordially invited to… front and back of a ticket for '79's "fayre", 1979.

Opposite left, top: A wholefoods food truck, 1979-style.

Opposite left, middle: A view of the festival site, 1979.

Opposite right: The camping site was mixed with the car park in those days, 1979.

Opposite bottom: Tents were a much simpler affair in 1979.

## "Are you the fellow that started it all?"

Queen Elizabeth, to Michael Eavis,
when he received a CBE in 2007.

Opposite: Peter Gabriel and friends
rock the Pyramid, 1979.

Below: Psychedelic pop rockers Mother
Gong, 1979.

Left: As the sun sets, the audience sits, 1979.

# DECADE PLAYLIST: 1970s

1. **T-REX 'BY THE LIGHT OF A MAGICAL MOON'**
2. **DAVID BOWIE 'CHANGES' (LIVE)**
3. **HAWKWIND 'SILVER MACHINE'**
4. **QUINTESSENCE 'ST PANCRAS'**
5. **TRAFFIC 'GIMME SOME LOVIN'**
6. **PETER GABRIEL 'SOLSBURY HILL'**
7. **ARTHUR BROWN 'INTERNAL MESSENGER'**
8. **JOHN MARTYN 'HEAD AND HEART'**
9. **FAIRPORT CONVENTION 'DIRTY LINEN'**
10. **TERRY REID 'SILVER WHITE LIGHT'**

**1980s**

FOLLOWING THE STRIFE AND CHAOS OF THE LARGELY EXPERIMENTAL 1979 FESTIVAL, GLASTONBURY RETURNED IN 1981 AS A LARGE-SCALE, EFFICIENTLY ORGANIZED EVENT WITH HEADLINE ARTISTS WHO WERE CONTRACTUALLY OBLIGED TO TURN UP. LIKE MOST OF THE COUNTRY, THE ARRIVAL OF THE 1980S SAW GLASTONBURY GO THROUGH A SHIFT IN PRIORITIES, CULMINATING IN THE FESTIVAL'S ASSOCIATION WITH CND, THE CREATION OF THE ENVIRONMENTALLY MINDED GREEN FIELDS, AND THE APPEARANCE OF POPULAR INDIE ROCK GROUPS PERFORMING ON A SHINY NEW PYRAMID STAGE. BUT, THIS WAS GLASTONBURY, SO MAGIC, MUD AND MAYHEM WERE NEVER FAR AWAY…

Glastonbury Festival returned better than ever on 19–21 June 1981. This time out, there was the Pyramid Stage that we know and love today. From this festival onwards, the Pyramid Stage would remain a permanent structure at Worthy Farm, doubling as a cowshed and food store for the rest of the year. The stage was no longer made of corrugated iron and plastic. In 1981, as Michael exclaimed, "the Pyramid Stage is clad in Ministry of Defence specification steel. It's supposed to be for lining ammunition dumps." In the context of the festival's CND association, the irony of this fact was not lost on Michael.

Andrew Kerr and Arabella Churchill returned to Worthy Farm and helped Michael secure the bounty licences that were now required for the event. The local council had got wise to the festival and had two eyes squarely set on Michael to ensure he would not break their rules.

Over the next six years, the number of people attending the festival would triple – from 18,000 people in 1981 to 60,000 in 1987. "It's very big now," Andrew Kerr said in 1981. "It got too big. It was time for the professionals to come in, I'm not a professional site manager. I thought it was too big in 1971, so you can imagine what I think about it now. It's still there to celebrate the summer solstice, and that was the main reason." In order to secure interest from the CND, Michael promised the organization that the festival would be professionally managed in order to turn a profit. It was the birth of his youngest daughter, Emily, which altered Michael's priorities for the festival and made him reach out to CND, a cause close to the festival's core "love and peace" ideals. "Emily's birth made me feel terribly protective. It made me think hard about CND, and I decided I wanted to do something with them," Michael told the *Observer* in 1981. This meant that Michael had to take control of the festival preparations and financial affairs far more fastidiously than in previous years. Accordingly, the 1981 fayre had all the size and scope of a large festival – including craft stalls, workshops, play parks for children, mime troupes and performance artists – all of which cost the festival goer £13 each, to cover Michael's costs. Too expensive for hippies, perhaps, but not for more politically minded festival-goers and teenagers with money from the bank of mum and dad. The festival also attracted "New Age travellers", as they became known, who found sanctuary there for most of the decade. Sadly they did not pay to get in, which resulted in numerous clashes that somewhat blotted the festival's love and peace vibe over a period of years.

The 1981 festival cost Michael Eavis £65,000 in total. He told the *Observer* in 1981 that his two main priorities for the newly devised event were that "everyone gets paid" and that the festival was more than just a rock festival. It had to mean something. "I wanted to do something in the medieval spirit, something *everyone* would enjoy and not just the stereotypical rock fan."

The Eighties was a period of major political upheaval in the United Kingdom, and for many of the tens of thousands of revellers that turned up at Worthy Farm in that decade, listening to rock music by wealthy stars was the very last thing on their minds. For perennial performer and LeftField organizer Billy Bragg, the politics of Glastonbury was what made the festival truly stand out. "In the 1980s, it was a gathering place for those of us who opposed Margaret Thatcher," Michael Eavis told the *Guardian*. "When Maggie came to power in '79, that was huge for us. Everybody had somewhere to go, you know, to get away from the Maggie thing in 1979 – the miners' strike and all that stuff. And closing down the pits and being hard on the working class and all that kind of thing. That's partly why we were so successful through the Eighties."

Michael Eavis's own sense of political loyalty developed before and during his stint in the Navy, prior to returning to Somerset. "My politics were influenced by working as a coalminer for a couple of years at Mendip Colliery when I first took over the farm," Michael told the *Guardian*. "I used to milk in the morning, and then go and do the day shift on the coal face, just to earn some money. I was a member of the National Union of Mineworkers, and the miners were all very left-wing. It gave me experience of dealing with working-class kids, and funnily enough I think that's what made the festival successful. Without that experience I could certainly never have handled the 50,000 New Age travellers who descended on us after the Battle of the Beanfield at Stonehenge [a clash between Stonehenge travellers and security guards] in 1985."

The festival's liberal and largely left-wing political aspirations made it the ideal summer vacation spot for those wishing to get away from the madness of Westminster. Sadly, those who made the long trip to Somerset from the city in midsummer 1981 may have been equally confused by the festival's headline acts, which comprised an eclectic roster of bands, including: Aswad, Decline and Fall, Gong, Gordon

Giltrap, Ginger Baker, Hawkwind, John Cooper Clarke, Judy Tzuke, Matumbi, Nick Pickett, Robert Hunter, Roy Harper, Supercharge, Taj Mahal, Talisman, New Order, Rab Noakes, The Jazz Sluts, The Sound, Hinkleys Heroes, Beverley Martin, Chicken Shack and Pete Drummond.

The odd ones out – newly formed, electro-rock upstarts New Order – shared the same night's bill as the old guard: hippie space rockers, and Glastonbury favourites, Hawkwind. The billing was beginning to highlight the organizer's increasing desire to mix the old with the new. "Listening to Radio One while I'm milking has helped me to choose the bands," Michael would admit. The BBC's Radio One has always championed new music, at the risk of losing old listeners.

Somewhat surprisingly, New Order's headline gig on the Saturday night went down as one of the worst starring gigs in the festival's history. However, there were some mitigating circumstances. In 1981, New Order were one of the UK's biggest bands, rising out of the ashes of Joy Division, following the suicide of that band's lead singer, Ian Curtis, in May 1980. Snagging New Order to play Glastonbury was a huge coup for Michael Eavis, as the band were expecting to return to chart glory with their debut album *Movement*, three months after their Glastonbury performance.

"Us and Hawkwind was quite a surreal coupling," recalled New Order's bassist, Peter Hook to the *NME*. "But I was actually happy with it because I was a Hawkwind fan as a kid. I remember it being a very loose and easy-going festival in those days, nice and relaxed. I remember going to Michael's house beforehand because the dressing room we had was a very cold, damp caravan. He suggested that we use his house instead and it was lovely."

Unfortunately for Bernard Sumner, New Order's newly installed singer, the near-headline spot proved to be too much pressure. To combat the stage fright of performing to a crowd who just wanted to hear "Love Will Tear Us Apart" (but left empty-handed), Sumner chose instead to get drunk. The group's drummer Steve Morris entertained the *Guardian* with how the gig unravelled into chaos. "Bernard rather over-imbibed on Pernod and halfway through one song just completely fell over and started playing guitar on his back," Morris revealed. "As a performer you have to draw the line between enjoying the festival and keeping yourself in a fit state to play."

Thankfully, Sumner's incapacity to play any tune went unnoticed by the crowd, which was mainly made up of "bikers who were ripping round the place at breakneck speed and revving their engines", according to Peter Hook. "It was definitely a pretty frosty reception, because everyone was waiting for Hawkwind. They were more Greasers rather than Hells Angels. I suppose it was our version of Altamont, but without any trouble."

The mayhem on the headline stage was not the only fracas between bands that year. Earlier in the weekend, a clash between Roy Harper and Ginger Baker had also ended up in mild fisticuffs. "I'm playing the gig, going down quite well, building up to the finale," Harper recalls. "Then Ginger starts walking on with drums, setting up right in front of me, destroying everything. I couldn't believe it. So I left the microphone and said 'Hey, what you doing?' And he said, 'Fuck off, you've been on here too fucking long...' and his band started bringing all their gear on."

Evidence that the festival was changing for the better came with the delivery of new "proper toilets" to Worthy Farm for the 1983 festival, bought from the proceeds of the 1981 and 1982 events. Nevertheless, as Howard Marks (AKA Mr Nice) commented, "The loos are a problem I can't ever see being solved." He was right at the time.

Having survived five prosecutions brought by Mendip District Council in 1984 – for breach of licensing conditions – Michael Eavis was on an Arthurian quest to show everyone just how vital the festival could be. If only everyone could just get along...

The billing of two opposing headliners – one commercial, one old school, like New Order and Hawkwind – was the start of a learning curve for the organizers. In 1984 this culminated in the decision to book the biggest band in the world at that time – the Smiths – effectively declaring that the festival's hippie ideals of the Seventies were now a thing of the past.

"It really started in 1984 with the Smiths," Eavis recalled to *M* magazine. "The old hippies wanted Santana and that kind of thing, but I knew we had to move on. We're a British festival, and we made a conscious decision to move towards pop music and fashionable British bands. I went up to Bristol University to see the Smiths play, and I was completely gobsmacked by the change of sound. I booked them right then. When they went on stage at Glastonbury, people were

> **"There was quite a lot of trouble with hippies and travellers. They looked like Sesame Street characters – sort of Russell Brand-looking people. It was scary – people round here aren't used to seeing people looking like that, behaving badly. Lots of drugs. I was a bit scared, too."** Michael Eavis

running towards the stage – it was so heart-warming. We've never looked back".

Glastonbury fans, "the stereotypical rock fans" (as Michael called them) were not happy that the festival organizers had seemingly betrayed them by "selling out" the ideology of the old guard in favour of chart-friendly, commercial indie-rock. The addition of the Smiths – alongside the Waterboys, Elvis Costello and Ian Dury and the Blockheads – to the line-up sparked a debate for the first time among "die-hard" Glastonbury fans about who should play the festival and who shouldn't: the debate still rages on even today.

Whatever your point of view, the Smiths playing Glastonbury in 1984 is widely regarded today, as it was at the time, as the first real turning point and major change in fortunes for the festival. "We think that Jay-Z [in 2008] was controversial, but the Smiths was so controversial on the same level in 1984," Emily Eavis told the *Guardian*. "A lot of people who expected Hawkwind every year really wanted it and fought for that. They didn't believe that the Smiths should be playing," recalled Michael Eavis of the Smiths' set, which he regards as one of the most influential in history. "People were going 'What's happened to Santana, then?' I said, 'This is not Santana, this is the Smiths.' They didn't like it."

Unlike New Order's set of 1981 – during which the band were largely ignored by the old rockers at the front of the stage – for the Smiths' show, younger fans rushed the stage, desperate to see their new favourite band, in what would become the first Pyramid Stage invasion. "When they started playing people started rushing towards the stage, Morrissey was actually beckoning the fans up on stage," Michael recalled. "When I saw that, I knew that the whole thing had changed into something else... there was no place for the Santana audience any longer. We'd gone into pop."

"It's not something that I'd like to relive," Morrissey actually recounts about that moment. "It wasn't the best of our performances, and there was some animosity from certain sectors of the crowd. It is quite strange when you're singing to people who obviously do not like you. People are there to see other groups, it's tricky, and that's how Glastonbury worked out for us." The Smiths gig descended into anarchy and the band were unable to finish their set. Lead guitarist Johnny Marr described the event most aptly, to the *NME*:

"Glastonbury's rise in popularity has a lot to do with rave culture. People were getting together in warehouses at the end of motorways just to avoid the police, and then they realized Glastonbury offered thousands of people a chance to get together legally. Suddenly, Glastonbury no longer seemed an outdated idea, whereas in the Eighties, it had been caught between the ideals of the Seventies and something which had yet to be defined."

## EVERYTHING IS CHANGING

Live music – and the broadcasting of live music – changed dramatically after the groundbreaking Live Aid event in 1985, which brought the chronic poverty and starvation in Ethiopia to the attention of the world. Live music and going to gigs suddenly became one of the most important and common social events for the "disaffected youth" of the western world. The Glastonbury Festival was there in just the right place and at just the right time to fix their fix. The 1985 event saw the size of the site increased by another 100 acres, enveloping the neighbouring Cockmill farm land, which was purchased by Michael Eavis as the festival was now welcoming more than 40,000 revellers each year.

Following the chaotic events of 1984, Michael and his growing team of organizers believed that 1985 was the time to do the festival justice and do it properly. "We'd been going half-cocked until then, breaking even and not making any money," Eavis said at the time. "After Stonehenge was closed to the public [in 1985], we had 50,000 people come down to Glastonbury instead. All that Stonehenge stuff, the hippies, the creativity, they all came down to my lovely farm. It was the middle of the Margaret Thatcher years, there was a lot of discontent." These "New Age travellers" would come to present a problem for Michael and the festival in a few years, culminating in the Battle of Yeoman's Bridge in 1990, when the travellers clashed with the festival's security team, resulting in injuries on both sides.

The 1985 festival was the first to receive much media attention for the sheer abundance of mud (made famous by comedian Alexei Sayle's quip, "a contact lens has been reported missing, could you look out for it?"). Now charged £16 per head for the pleasure of attending, revellers got much more than they bargained for, as the heavens opened all weekend and everyone got a thorough soaking.

Over the next decade, the festival's expansion and transformation gradually revealed themselves with the arrival of new stages and events in the fields of Worthy Farm. These included the classical tent curated by composer John Williams, in 1986, alongside the West Holts stage, the Mutoid Waste Company structures, sculptures and exhibitions, and even a Guinness World Record attempt. This was in the art of juggling when, on 26 June 1984, 826 people juggled at least three objects all at once, and managed to keep all 2,478 objects in the air simultaneously. It was the first, but not the last, record that Glastonbury has set.

The end of the decade was a period that witnessed Glastonbury becoming larger than ever expected – and in more surprising ways than ever imagined – with more than 65,000 paying punters. This growth and diversification hinted at the complex and compelling future that awaited the festival in the 1990s and beyond.

1989 saw major headline acts such as Hothouse Flowers, the Waterboys, Van Morrison, Suzanne Vega (dressed in a bulletproof vest, following a death threat), The Pixies, Donovan, The Wonderstuff, Youssou N'Dour, Elvis Costello, Alexei Sayle and others, all rubbing shoulders among the various stages. However, it was activity away from the main stages, in the distant corners of the event, that was to signal the future of the festival. In the far-flung fields of Worthy Farm, scores of thousands of New Age travellers enjoyed a new type of sound echoing around the fields: electronic house music – played on large sound systems that rivalled the systems used on the main stages. This new music was to become the soundtrack of the early part of the Nineties, and Glastonbury would once again have to redefine its identity in order to remain relevant. As Michael Eavis has often said, "The festival is subject to fashion – it could come and go in a wink, 200,000 people could decide it's not fashionable any more." At this point in the life of the festival, all Michael had to do was find a way of bringing everyone together, old and new, as new musical genres were bursting to the foreground, fighting for space with what had gone before. "We've got different creeds and different beliefs and stuff, but there is a common thread there and it all comes together at Glastonbury. That's why it works. That's why it works."

Right: Covered in mud, circa 1985.

Above: Michael Eavis makes a wish in front
of the Pyramid Stage, circa 1985.

Opposite above: Stargazing in the Glastonbury
fields is top notch, 1980s.

Opposite below: Asleep in a gateway in
Pilton, circa 1985.

Opposite: Music, motorcycles, mud and a man wearing a paper hat, mid-80s.

Below: Lost and Found, the Message Kiosk, mid-80s.

"It was quite unpredictable in the early '80s, it wasn't anything like it is now." Emily Eavis

Above left: The CND was Glastonbury's chosen
beneficiary throughout the 80s.

Above right: Music fans bathe (and broil) in the
sunshine, 1982.

Opposite: The times (and fashions) they are
a-changing, 1982.

Above: A piece of peace for a pound, 1983.

Opposite above: The fight for fresh water... an ongoing concern, 1982.

Opposite below: Ice cream dreams, 1983.

Above: Until the late 1980s, festival goers could camp close to the stage.

Below: A vendor sells peace of mind, circa 1985.

Opposite: Legendary bassist, Robbie Shakespeare, from Sly and Robbie, performed on stage with Jackson Browne, 1982.

Above left: Jamaican reggae providers Aswad headline the Pyramid, 1983.

Above right: Alexei Sayle makes his famous contact lens quip on stage.

Below: A punk with a Mohican powers down for the afternoon, 1983.

# THE GREEN FIELDS

1984 was a bumper year for change at Glastonbury. While the Pyramid Stage saw off its inaugural invasion, something much quieter and more polite was going on in the Green Fields. This was a new network of interconnected fields with environmentally friendly, renewable-energy food and creative stalls and workshops, promoting a one-ness with the Earth and its peoples. Inset within the now-60 acres of Green Fields are the Healing Fields, Green Futures, and the Greenpeace Field, offering visitors an environmental education and a break for their ears away from the Pyramid Stage. However, the origins of the Green Fields actually lay in nuisance, rather than nobility. The Green Collective had been coming to the Glastonbury area since 1980, organizing "Green Gatherings" at the same time as Glastonbury to promote the glory of Mother Nature, but the two events were not directly connected.

In 1983, Michael Eavis asked the Green Collective to move on from the festival, as he was under pressure from Mendip council. They were on the hunt for reasons to fine Michael to the hilt, arguing that any smaller gatherings on the farm – not associated with the festival – would be in breach of the licensing conditions

at his festival and make him liable for prosecution. The Green Collective and Michael came to an agreement – they could stay, but they would have to become part of the festival.

Today, the Green Fields is one of the most popular areas within the festival. Home to the Kings Meadow, the festival's most sacred space, and site of the Stone Circle (where the sunrises are epic), the Green Fields offer one of the best views of the entire site. Also to be found at the Green Fields is the Peace Dome, which burns the eternal flame that was lit from the atomic fires of Hiroshima in 1945. This symbol of forgiveness and unity combines with the Peace Garden and the Healing Fields, where you can find your own spiritual awakening with a host of healers and therapists. Finally, at the Tipi Field, you can celebrate different world traditions and cultures all in one place. In 1985, following the success of the previous year, the Green Fields expanded and have been doing so every year since. Apart from everything else they have to offer, the Green Fields host the secret Underground Piano Bar that Michael Eavis sings at every year, but whose location is never printed on maps of the festival site.

Right top: Music fans phone home, standard rates apply. 1985.

Right middle: Just one week after 1985's Live Aid concert, Bob Geldof and the Boomtown Rats perform at Glastonbury.

Right bottom: 1985 – one of the first famously muddy years. But by no means the last.

Opposite: Cruising in to the ticket checkpoint, 1984.

"In the past I've used a rowing boat to paddle through a lake full of excrement and fish out rubbish with my hands." Michael Eavis

Top left: All cops are bastards: a growing number of scuffles between police and travellers began to upset the organizers.

Top right: The Pogues performing at Glastonbury, 1986.

Above: The security fence in front of the stage collapses, though it was only a picket fence. 1986.

Below: 1987 – a changing crowd for a changing festival.

# DECADE PLAYLIST: 1980s

1. **BOOMTOWN RATS 'I DON'T LIKE MONDAYS'**
2. **NEW ORDER 'DENIAL'**
3. **VAN MORRISON 'SUMMERTIME IN ENGLAND'**
4. **IAN DURY 'HIT ME WITH YOUR RHYTHM STICK'**
5. **ELVIS COSTELLO 'OLIVER'S ARMY'**
6. **BILLY BRAGG 'THERE IS POWER IN A UNION'**
7. **THE SMITHS 'THIS CHARMING MAN'**
8. **THE CURE 'BOYS DON'T CRY'**
9. **SUZANNE VEGA 'LUKA'**
10. **MADNESS 'BAGGY TROUSERS'**

Left top: Rhode Island's pioneers of raucous rock, Throwing Muses, 1989.

Left middle: Youssou N'Dour's eclectic brand of solar-powered Senegalese music was a surprise hit with the congregation in the Jazz World field, 1989.

Left bottom: Mike Scott of the Waterboys, one of Glastonbury's most frequent flyers, 1989.

Opposite: The Mutoid Waste Company's Joe Rush and Robin Cooke, who conceived and designed Arcadia's famous flaming 'spider' not long after, 1989.

1990S | FUTURE HISTORY

GFMC1990-9/66-97

IT'S PERHAPS NO SURPRISE THAT THE ERA OF "GOLDEN GLASTONBURY" ARRIVED AT THE SAME TIME AS SEVERAL NEW MUSICAL GENRES. EVERYBODY WAS LISTENING TO EVERYTHING, BECAUSE THERE WAS SO MUCH MORE OF EVERYTHING TO LISTEN TO. IN THIS DECADE ALONE, AN EXPLOSION OF INDIE ROCK, ELECTRO, BRITPOP, BOY BANDS, SOUL AND R&B, GRUNGE, HIP HOP, RAP AND HOUSE ALL BEGAN FIGHTING IN THE POP CHARTS – NO LONGER DOMINATED BY JUST POP. GLASTONBURY, REMAINED AHEAD OF THE CURVE WHEN IT CAME TO SHOWCASING NEW MUSIC, POP CULTURE, ART AND FASHION – HOLDING UP A MIRROR TO THE CHANGING TASTES OF A CHANGING SOCIETY.

Michael Eavis's vision of Glastonbury remaining a place where "love and peace" came together was shattered in the early years of the Nineties. The scores of thousands of "New Age Stonehenge travellers" and gatecrashers (numbers reaching more than 100,000) that had once found free sanctuary courtesy of Michael at the festival, were now causing the founder too many headaches with the local council, and threatening the future of his creation. Something had to be done. It all came to a head in 1990 at the Battle of Yeoman's Bridge, where a major scuffle between police, security and the convoys of travellers took place. This was the straw that broke the camel's back and forced the organizers to abandon Glastonbury 1991. They needed a wall to keep people out in order to keep those inside safe.

When the festival returned in 1992 – at the height of grunge and "baggy" indie rock – the travellers were no longer allowed in for free, and a 3-metre (10-foot) high steel fence was erected around the perimeter. This major change marked the beginning of an era of tightened security at Glastonbury. Having said that, until the even bigger "super fence" was built in 2002, thousands of gatecrashers still enjoyed all the fun of the festival for free. Die-hard festival fans regarded any entrance fences at all to be a step too far away from the original ideals of the festival. As for Michael Eavis, he simply wanted to protect the safety of the punters who had paid to have the best times of their lives. It was an ugly time in the festival's history, and one which caused Michael much anxiety, not least because he was fighting an unwinnable war. "I've been critical of Glastonbury in the past," claimed The Levellers' singer Mark Chadwick, "like in 1992 when Michael Eavis cut off the travellers' field. They were nomads, they were refugees from the law, and Michael put the kybosh on it. I got very cross at the time, but I've spoken to him since and I realize he didn't have a choice."

Musically, the 1990 festival – marking the twentieth anniversary of the event – was a blinder: vintage Glastonbury. The nation's best purveyors of baggy, the Happy Mondays, headlined alongside goth-rockers The Cure, while Sinead O' Connor, James, Jesus Jones, Ry Cooder, World Party and De La Soul highlighted Glastonbury's desire to traverse the entire spectrum of sound. 1990 was also the year that the festival changed its name to "The Glastonbury Festival of Contemporary Performing Arts". This was a declarative statement that showed the world the festival wasn't just about the music – it was about everything. "I thought it was important that the festival had a cross-section of the arts," said Michael. "From the beginning, there's always been something to fight against but now more than ever, with the arts cuts and the current government, there are things to talk about. It's important that Glastonbury fights for something," Michael told *M* magazine.

As if to prove a point about how far the festival had come in terms of artistry, the French theatre troupe Archaos performed atop the Pyramid Stage on both Friday and Saturday nights, deploying the first ever laser show at Glastonbury. 70,000 people's minds were duly blown.

The year also began the decade-long promise to Green charities, such as new partners Greenpeace (who received £250,000 in donations this year alone – all profit from the event) and Oxfam. The nuclear threat was no longer relevant, and so the festival ceased its connection with CND.

The Nineties also saw the festival expand in size and ambition with the invention of Arcadia, Lost Vagueness, the *NME* Stage, the Other Stage, the Dance Tent, the Glade Area and the Stone Circle in Kings Meadow. For Michael, the addition of the new stages and fields is a reward to the loyal punters who come each year. Every year offers something new, even if the festival has now grown to a size and scale that even its founder can no longer comprehend. "It's all crazy, isn't it? I mean it's all a bit Mad Max wherever you go, it's all outrageous really. I can't think of anything that's not outrageous," Michael told the *Guardian*.

One of the most popular new additions was the permanent booking of comedians to appear on stage. Arguably, the most perennial is Bill Bailey, who has yet to miss a festival since 1993 (though he lives in Somerset, so has no excuse not to go!), and one day hopes to headline. "It's Glastonbury, so anything could happen."

When Glastonbury returned in 1992, the shift in the musical zeitgeist was apparent. Just not on the Pyramid Stage. Yet. That was still home to the big bands such as Carter USM, Shakespears Sister, Primal Scream, P J Harvey, Sawdoctors and The Levellers. 1992 also saw the development of the Jazzworld Stage, which rewarded visitors with world music and a cacophony of jazz.

Rave culture – which had begun at the end of the Eighties in the far-flung fields of the festival, on illicitly imported sound systems – was now a serious part of the youth scene. It definitely required its own space at the festival. Glastonbury had previously allowed raves to set up, even exploring the possibility of an "anarchic techno Experimental Sound Field", though it never actually came to fruition. The zenith of this new dance craze arrived with Orbital's seminal, groundbreaking set in 1994. This laid the way for the Dance Tent, which first appeared in 1995, officially giving "electronic music" a permanent home on site at Glastonbury.

The now-iconic Sunday afternoon Legacy artist or "Oldie spot" started in the mid-Nineties, where artists such as Tom Jones, Johnny Cash ("I love you people!"), Tony Bennett, James Taylor, Page and Plant, Bob Dylan and Al Green rejuvenated their declining careers with much success. Cash's set, in particular, ignited Michael Eavis's passions. "I booked Johnny Cash to play at Glastonbury in 1994. He was one of my best bookings of all time. This was when Johnny wasn't nearly as fashionable as he was after 'Hurt'. Some of the youngsters thought I'd gone crazy, as they believed I should be booking new stuff all the time. They thought he was just a daft old country singer. But he was so good." Even Cash would later claim the set to be one of his favourite. Today, this Sunday afternoon slot is one of the most anticipated sets of the weekend.

## 1994 – NEED WE SAY MORE?

As Glastonbury approached the mid-Nineties, the festival began to enter a vintage period. Paul Weller said it best: "By the mid-Nineties, Glastonbury Festival had abandoned its hippie roots and become a perfect cultural barometer for British culture."

In 1994, Glastonbury reached parts that other festivals couldn't reach and went truly global. This was largely due to two groundbreaking sets by Orbital and Oasis – bands that were soon to be culturally significant across the world. Yes, The Levellers would also play to (apparently) the biggest crowd ever recorded at Glastonbury, on the Friday headline slot – but with the gatecrashers a bigger problem than ever before, does it count? Numbers have never been confirmed, though a total figure of 300,000 has been touted within the media. This is possible, as The Levellers – with their bohemian hippie-based

folk-rock melodies – are the perfect Glastonbury band. "I don't know whether we evoke the spirit of the festival more than any other band" singer Mark Chadwick said, "but we have been playing Glasto for 20 years".

1994 was a stellar year for the festival, if not for its founder, or the Pyramid Stage. Before the well-received event kicked off, Michael underwent bowel cancer surgery, a "life-saving operation". More than ever, Michael needed Glastonbury. "Music from favourites such as Van Morrison and Ray Charles helped pull me through," he said. Sadly, the Pyramid Stage burned down a week before the festival kicked off, on 13 June 1994, requiring a replacement makeshift stage to be quickly erected so that the festival could go ahead. Michael Eavis is not a fan of dance music, per se, so the ascension of dance music at Glastonbury in the early Nineties baffled him at first. With that said, he was responsible for the headline booking of Orbital on the *NME* Stage on Saturday night – a brave choice, a masterstroke in retrospect, that perfectly took the temperature of the country.

"I don't actually like electronic music," Michael told the *Guardian*. "We've changed as fashions change, and in a way we've just tried to follow the trends of youth culture. Actually, I tried to stick to the stuff I like, but people wanted more of this or that, and then my kids would say, 'We like dance music, we want a dance village!' I'd say, 'Aww, but I don't like it though!' and they'd reply 'It's not about you, it's about us!' So we've changed things like that. My own tastes are not diverse, not really," Michael admitted to the *Guardian*.

Orbital's set at Glastonbury 1994 changed everything. The festival had yet to define itself for the danceheads, remaining a traditional "guitar-based" festival, and indeed 1994's line-up was packed with an entire weekend of six stringers, including the Manic Street Preachers, Oasis, Radiohead, the Boo Radleys and Blur. Orbital were very much a band perfectly placed to cleanse the aural palate.

Like the Smiths before them – who played their innovative set a full decade earlier – it was Orbital's fresh-sounding, drum and bass, techno-based performance in 1994 that heralded a new age at Glastonbury. It's what the kids wanted, after all. "What was previously underground made it on to one of the big stages, and there was no going back from there," said Michael of Orbital's trance-inducing sound.

**"I love putting it together. I get a real buzz out of it. It gets better every time, that's why when people ask me for my favourite year I can never say. As for the future, I just hope the event can improve the quality of people's lives and the aspirations of people who haven't got a lot going on. I'd like to think it could inspire people with a vision of what they can do."** Michael Eavis

Channel 4, the first broadcasters of the festival before the BBC bought the television rights in 1997, was at Glastonbury that year and televised a portion of the gig. For the first time, Orbital's Phil and Paul Hartnoll's torch headlight "stage costume" was on show. This was both practical and visually stimulating – if confusing to the millions of armchair festival-goers who may never have had the opportunity to see an Orbital show, let alone go to a dance club. The show was *insta*-iconic. Even the band knew it, as they walked offstage to wild, rapturous applause: "At the end we did the dance we used to do when we were little kids and naked and about to get in the bath," exclaimed Paul, "banging our bottoms together and laughing. It was just brilliant. It was like, we've made it." Michael's youngest daughter, Emily Eavis, who was about 14 at the time, called out Orbital's gig as "one of the all-time great Glastonbury sets".

Orbital made such a vital first impression on Michael that, somewhat unsurprisingly, the aforementioned Dance Tent was ordered for the 1995 festival, positioned in the Glade Area. With this seminal move, Glastonbury gave rave culture an official stamp of approval. The country swiftly followed suit. "As the police and the council made me very well aware, the buzz had been around the raves and the market sound systems and in the travellers' fields for years. But it needed a showcase to make it legal." Within ten years the newly installed Glade Area replaced the Avalon Field and grew from one dance tent (capacity 1,500) in 1995 to the dance village, in 2004, which can now hold more than 20,000 people. In 2013, the whole field was revamped and called "Silver Hayes".

## RULE BRITANNIA

While Orbital were making and breaking ground with their dance music, Britpop was dominating the *NME* Stage (renamed the "Other Stage" in 1997) and the Pyramid Stage in all its glorious forms. As former *NME* scribe Mark Beaumont reported, "The first moment that Britpop gelled into a recognizable movement was when we gazed down the running order of the Other Stage [sic] at Glastonbury on Sunday, 26 June 1994. Blur, Oasis, Pulp, Radiohead – a sharp new gang was in town." Radiohead's Jonny Greenwood would agree: "We were on between Oasis and Blur. What a line-up - it was like the Champions League."

First up to break the mould was Oasis's era-defining performance from fifth from the bottom of the bill on the Sunday. As Oasis ripped into 'Shakermaker' – the first of their eight-song set – Liam Gallagher sneered at what he perceived still to be the great unwashed. "Are you lot gonna wake up then?" he snarled, "for some proper songs?" Britpop had landed.

"I remember Oasis in 1994 were absolutely brilliant and we'd never heard of them really," remembers Michael. "That was the best set they've ever done in their lives. All the bands tend to play better here than people are expecting them to, don't you think? Not 1995 or any later, because they... deteriorated with age, I think. But they were fantastic in 1994."

Oasis would return as world champions in 1995 (with their ill-fated collaboration with a "shit-faced" Robbie Williams), though it was Pulp's replacement headline gig that hogged all the glory that year. Oasis performed at Glastonbury again in 2004, ten years after their legendary first time. Although, apparently, against their will... "I fucking hate Glastonbury. I'm only here for the money. It's fucking shit. I've got to wear fucking wellies," Liam Gallagher told anyone who would listen. Noel Gallagher kept the peace: "Glastonbury is the only real festival, the best. The rest of them are just rock bands playing in fields."

Rumours of an Oasis reunion have abounded over the years, prompting Noel Gallagher to comment to Q magazine. "Nobody has made us an offer. But if I was ever going to do it, it would only be for the money. This isn't me putting it out there, by the way. Would I do it for charity? No way. We're not that kind of people. For Glastonbury? I don't think Michael Eavis has got enough money. But would we get back together one day? As long as everybody is still alive and still has their hair, it's always a possibility. But only for the money." Over to you, Michael...

Speaking of 1995, much praise must be heaped on Pulp, who that year proved to be the little band that really could do the business. When John Squire, the lead guitarist of the Stone Roses, fell off his bike and broke his leg, Pulp bravely stepped in to replace the legendary Mancunian outfit. They were not immediately thought of as heirs to the throne – Blur, Primal Scream and Rod Stewart were all allegedly approached beforehand – but Jarvis Cocker's gang actually said "yes".

In an interview with *NME* just a few days before the show, Jarvis discussed the importance of the impending gig: "With it being the 25th Glastonbury, it's a chance to participate in a culturally significant event, something that people will remember for a long time. No, I don't think we'll be doing any Stone Roses covers." On stage, Jarvis wowed and won the crowd, becoming a common man of the people in the process. "Pulp's performance that night was very good," Michael said afterwards to the *Guardian*. "Jarvis was always going to go down well here because he's an eccentric – eccentric artists go down well at Glastonbury because we're an eccentric mob. I remember liking 'Common People', though I think I've heard enough of it now."

## 1997: THE YEAR OF THE MUD

"I've never seen mud like it in my whole life, it hasn't been as bad as this," said Michael Eavis of his Glastonbury Festival in 1997, now known colloquially as the "Year of the Mud". Torrential rain drowned the site the weekend before, but enthusiastic revellers were not to be put off. If anything, the mud made the festival the most memorable event in years.

Photographs of revellers dancing and partying (and surviving) in the sludge and muck made headlines around the world, and the image has been key to the public perception of the festival ever since. It is just possible that it is the legendary mud that has cemented the idea that the Glastonbury Festival is the world's greatest, and truly original, summer happening. Glastonbury isn't just a music festival – it is an *experience*.

With its incredible line-up of international acts, iconic performances and now era-defining images of almost all the 90,000 festival-goers throwing mud at each other, Glastonbury 1997 saw more live performances than ever before. The site also expanded to more than 800 acres – with Michael Eavis acquiring yet more land to fill the demand. 1997 saw the introduction of the now famous Greenpeace Field, with its reconstructed *Rainbow Warrior* and solar-heated showers, as well as John Peel and Jo Whiley's first BBC2 coverage of the festival as presenters, taking over from Channel 4. This prime-time coverage would change the fortunes of the festival forever, turning every year into a globally televised event. "It's the biggest outside broadcasting that the BBC do," said Michael Eavis in 1997. "It's

bigger than Wimbledon. I mean it's huge, the coverage. The resources to get down here in the middle of a muddy field in Somerset and to set it all up costs a fortune." Whiley and Peel's Glastonbury coverage would go on to attract millions of viewers at home and become as watchable as any soap opera, thanks to the pair's riotous chemistry. "I just like coming here," Peel would say. "I like the atmosphere generally, I like some of the unsuitable and fattening foods that they serve. And incidentally, I quite like some of the music, but the music I have relegated almost to secondary importance to the event itself." Sadly, Peel passed away in 2004, but not before leaving a lasting impression. "John was what people think of when they think of Glastonbury," said Whiley. "He embodied what Glastonbury, the experience, should be about." Indeed, the John Peel Stage, championing new music, was devised in 2005. "It's very appropriate because it's all the sort of music that John would have chosen. He was a master at choosing the bands that were going to make it," Michael said, when announcing the stage.

But for all of Glastonbury 1997's mud, music and quality presenting, this year will go down in history for just one thing – Radiohead, and their era-defining headline performance on the Pyramid Stage.

## ALONG CAME RADIOHEAD

In 2006, readers of music magazine *Q* voted Radiohead's set at Glastonbury 1997 "the greatest gig of all time". Michael too revealed it to be in his top five favourite Glastonbury performances so far, calling it "the most inspiring festival gig in 30 years." John Peel famously disagreed, telling BBC viewers during his now iconic presenting of the event (which also began in 1997) that "I never could see what people saw in that band," much to the inflamed, but hilarious, annoyance of his co-presenter, Jo Whiley.

Despite Radiohead's performance being rapturously received in 1997 – and it is still just as highly regarded today – the band themselves loathed every second of the gig, blaming too many "technical failures". This was mainly due to the band's on stage monitors malfunctioning throughout their set, so that they were unable to hear or see properly.

Headlining Glastonbury for their first time, the decision to book Radiohead was an inspired act by Michael. The Oxfordshire group had released their third album, *OK Computer*, just two weeks previously. The record would come to define the paranoid and frustrated political and cultural angst of the pre-millennium era. The superficial substance of Britpop had been revealed. Reality had kicked in and Radiohead's set at Glastonbury was the alarm bell. "We felt very much like we had a huge spotlight on us in 1997," Colin Greenwood, the group's bassist recalled later. "*OK Computer* had just been released and went down very well, and suddenly we went from standing to being at some sort of enforced speed in a very short space of time." It's ironic then, that for their headline performance the band couldn't actually hear or see what they were doing.

"Can you turn on the lights so we can see the people. We haven't seen them yet," said frontman Thom Yorke to the lighting director, voicing the failure of the backline and front of house systems, among other woes. (Thom would repeat the line in 2017, 20 years later, when he wanted to see the crowd). "Everything broke on stage," Ed O'Brien, the band's guitarist, remembered, recoiling in terror. "It turned into the worst night of our lives. I don't think we ever wanted to play a concert again."

Dismayed and horrified that what should have been the biggest gig of their career was turning into a car crash live in front of 100,000 people, Thom Yorke decided it was probably for the best if he just left. "At one point I just went over to Ed. I tapped him on the shoulder and said, 'I'm off mate, see you later'. Ed turned around and went, 'If you do, you'll probably live the rest of your life regretting it'. I went, 'Good point' and carried on with the show." Thank goodness for Ed...

## FEAR AND LOVING IN LOST VAGUENESS

Over in the "naughty corner", or the south-easterly most point of the festival, was a new attraction for the masses to enjoy – Lost Vagueness. This, alongside Arcadia, was the next seismic shift in Glastonbury's identity. It arrived with rain and mud in 1997 and, for ten years, was revered as "Glastonbury's home of vaudevillian late-night excess". For the first time, Glastonbury had an after-hours entertainment area. This "festival within a festival" gave festival-goers a chance to experience balls (in ballgowns), poker tournaments, burlesque shows and, generally, satisfy their eyes and ears with all the entertainment that the Pyramid Stage couldn't offer – in short, debauchery. "Without Lost Vagueness, Glastonbury would have died", former operations director Melvin Benn said, hinting at the festival's

dire need to break free of the constraints of just being a music festival. "We weren't selling as many tickets before it," Michael admitted. "It was an anarchic, original idea that saved the Glastonbury festival at a difficult time". The area became as much of an attraction as any band or DJ, especially in the small hours of the morning once the Pyramid Stage had been emptied. "We weren't there to cause trouble, but we did cause trouble," said Lost Vagueness founder Roy Gurvitz.

After ten years, Lost Vagueness closed up shop, and was replaced by the Shangri-La in 2008, a new fantasy land that to this day offers punters and festival crew the chance to "return the festival to the spirit of its original 1970s incarnation," according to Shangri-La's creative director, Debs Armstrong. However, in 1997 Lost Vagueness wasn't Michael Eavis's only exploration into lunacy. With Lost Vagueness Glastonbury had its first after-hours area; with Arcadia, another new addition to the festival in 1997, Michael and the festival organizers offered a dystopian alternative to Lost Vagueness's carnivalesque fantasy land.

Today, Arcadia, or more pertinently "the spider", travels and tours all over the world. But its home will always be in the south-east field of Glastonbury. "Arcadia came to me and said they needed £20,000 to buy some cranes for sale from Southampton docks because they were going to build 'a spider'. I gave Pip (Rush) and Bert (Cole) the £20K – I didn't even know these two boys – but it's been a huge success," Michael informed the *Guardian*. "People are full of ideas," he continued, "and what's more, they can put them together and make them work. It's not hippie nonsense." The creators of Arcadia's famous flaming spider are, according to *The Independent*, "the frantically beating heart of Michael Eavis's annual shebang, where ravers go to storm the dancefloor as DJs spin sets amid dramatic pyrotechnics, awe-inspiring circus acts, cutting-edge technology and all-consuming sensory mayhem."

## END OF THE CENTURY

As the dawning of a new millennium rose above the fields of Worthy Farm, and the sunshine returned to the festival in 1999 to wave goodbye to the century, tragedy struck the Eavis family with the passing of "Mother Glastonbury", Michael's wife Jean Eavis, to cancer. A fireworks display and an illuminated wicker structure was offered to the gods in her honour, and REM's beautiful singalong track, 'Everybody Hurts', was sung to Jean as a tribute by the entire festival.

"To run the festival successfully requires teamwork, rolling up your sleeves and getting stuck in along with everyone else. This makes the work more fun and helps motivate everyone." Michael Eavis

"Jean was my moderator," said a devastated Michael. "She knew when I was going over the top, getting something wrong. She would rein me in, put me in my place." It was Jean who encouraged Michael to gatecrash the Bath Blues Festival with her and, in the process, "discovered hundreds of thousands of strange and interesting people, the like of whom we had never seen before." Without Jean, there would have been no Glastonbury.

With Jean's passing, it was another Eavis, Emily – the couple's daughter – who would come to help her father carry on the legacy of the festival and follow in her mother's giant footsteps. Emily, then aged 19, the same age Eavis was when his father died, remembers walking down to the Pyramid Stage for the minute's silence in honour of her mother. She paraded through thousands upon thousands of people, each one standing quiet. "I think people were very touched and really felt the enormity of the festival that year, and everything it stands for," Emily said. "There was a great feeling of togetherness."

In 1999, as Emily Eavis's time at the festival came to pass, by some serendipitous fate so did that of a fledging band who made their first appearance at the festival, admittedly to no great acclaim at the time. Their name was Coldplay. For the next 20 years, give or take, they would grow in stature alongside Emily's involvement in the festival to become the definitive Glastonbury band for a new millennium, becoming the only band ever to headline four times. With Emily by his side, Michael Eavis would transform the festival once again.

Right: Costumes have always been a big part of the Glastonbury experience, 1995.

Above: Suited and booted: Blur's 13-song set showed the band to be in a field of their own, 1992.

Below: With most of the crowd wearing *Screamadelica* t-shirts, it was clear that Bobby Gillespie's Primal Scream had arrived, 1992.

Opposite above: Festival goers occupy their time, circa 1990.

Opposite below: Sinead O' Connor's well-reviewed Glastonbury set bought Gaelic melodies to the festival.

Opposite: Playing the pipe of peace, 1992.

Below: Sunshine after the rain: a great way to commune with nature is to take a mud bath.

Bottom: Mid 90s: With tents finally pushed further away from the stage, it won't be long before a designated campsite, stage left of the Pyramid, is installed.

Above left: Naked, happy and covered in mud, 1993.

Above right: Richard Ashcroft of the Verve, 1993. They returned to Glastonbury in 2008.

Below: Wall and peace – the first fence, 1993.

Opposite: The Pyramid Stage burnt down just ten days before the festival was due to start in 1994. It would become a permanent structure from this point on.

"If you want something to happen enough then it actually will happen. And I believe that. In fact, that's why we're stood on this stage today… if a lanky git like me can do it, then you can do it too!" Jarvis Cocker

# HANGING OUT AT THE HENGE

The festival's sacred space, the Stone Circle, rose to prominence in 1992. The festival's own megalithic tribute to Stonehenge, and the summer solstice, the Stone Circle is the best place to see the sun rise and set across the festival site and as such has taken on a near mythical and spiritual place in Glastonbury revellers' hearts. The monument comprises 20 large stones laid out in a circle. Over the years, many other tribute "henges" have been installed, including Carhenge (1987), Banksy's Toilet-Henge (2007) – made out of reconstructed portaloos ("A lot of monuments are a bit rubbish, but this really is a pile of crap", said the artist) – not to be confused with Toilet-Gate (1999), the now famous war of words between Billy Bragg and the Manic Street Preachers' Nicky Wire ("I wouldn't let him piss in my toilet for all the money in the world," etc.) – Cubehenge (2010, see left) by Connected Cube and, of course Welly-Henge, which happens every time mud makes an appearance at the festival.

Above: Thom Yorke's Radiohead – arguably one of the festival's greatest ever gigs, 1997. Do you agree?

Opposite: Hanging out at the Stone Circle.

Above: The Cure's Robert Smith performs to one of the largest ever crowds, 1995.

Opposite above: Page and Plant, together again, 1995.

Opposite below: Phil Hartnoll of Orbital, 1995. Their inclusion marked dance music's arrival to the Glastonbury mainstream.

"The theme of this event so far has been mud, and it's good British mud at that." John Peel, 1997

Top: John and Jo, Peel and Whiley begin their BBC
coverage of the event, 1997.

Above: These boots were made for muddying, 1997.

Opposite: The muddiest year ever! Definitely
maybe, 1997.

Overleaf: Fans go wild, 1997.

Above: Naughty campers in Kings Meadow, 1997.

Below: The queue for soft ice cream was getting out of hand in 1997.

Opposite, clockwise from top: the Chemical Brothers, 1997; Keith Flint of the Prodigy on the Other Stage, 1995; Lenny Kravitz, Pyramid Stage 1999.

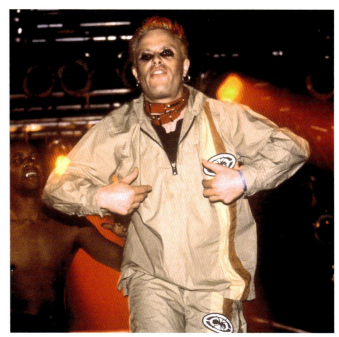

Left above: "Last time I was here I got fired," quipped Robbie Williams before belting out 'Angels' to a very wet Glastonbury.

Left below: Ian Brown, of the by-now-defunct Stone Roses, finally gets to perform at Glastonbury, 1998.

Opposite: Glastonbury at sunset. A sight to behold, 1998.

"We'd like to think it's the energy, spirit and community on the dancefloor. That's what it's always been about, both at Glastonbury and for us. Ultimately, massive spiders and 50-foot flames are conduits to harness and amplify those core elements. We've always seen our arena and our pyrotechnics as a modern interpretation of the primal concept of gathering around a campfire to celebrate. The fire's just got a bit bigger! We've also changed the bulk of our flame system to use recycled bio fuels (old chip fat) and obviously the structure is 99 per cent recycled, so I guess we're all hippies at heart!" Arcadia founders, Pip Rush & Bert Cole

# DECADE PLAYLIST: 1990s

1. **HAPPY MONDAYS 'STEP ON'**
2. **ORBITAL 'ARE WE HERE'**
3. **DE LA SOUL 'THE MAGIC NUMBER'**
4. **THE LEVELLERS 'ONE WAY'**
5. **UNDERWORLD 'BORN SLIPPY'**
6. **OASIS 'LIVE FOREVER'**
7. **PULP 'COMMON PEOPLE'**
8. **RADIOHEAD 'NO SURPRISES'**
9. **THE PRODIGY 'FIRESTARTER'**
10. **JOHNNY CASH 'A BOY NAMED SUE'**

Left: Courtney Love's Hole at Glastonbury, 1999.
Clothes were optional.

Opposite: By 1999, festival goers had been able to
build up quite a collection of wristbands.

2000s | A NEW MILLENNIUM

GFSB2000-9/98-129

BOLDLY GOING WHERE NO GLASTONBURY HAD GONE BEFORE, THE NOUGHTIES USHERED IN AN ERA IN WHICH THE FESTIVAL WAS NO LONGER AFRAID TO BE FEARLESS. THE IMPLEMENTATION OF THE "RING OF STEEL SUPER FENCE" AND THE TICKET REGISTRATION SYSTEM SHOWED THAT THE EAVIS FAMILY – AND THE MEAN FIDDLER MUSIC PROMOTION GROUP – WERE NOT SCARED TO PLAY BY THE RULES. THE FESTIVAL CONTINUED TO EXPAND AND EVOLVE WITH THE ADVENT OF BLOCK 9 (ONE WORD: MAYHEM), THE LEFTFIELD ARENA, THE THEATRE AND CIRCUS FIELDS AND THE BRAND NEW (THIRD) PYRAMID STAGE, FOUR TIMES BIGGER THAN THE ORIGINAL.

## LET'S ALL MEET UP IN THE YEAR 2000

The new millennium dawned at Glastonbury with an absolutely banging festival. It was the year 2000. David Bowie was the main draw, in a roster of artists that was perhaps less than stellar. At the time, Bowie was performing his Earthling tour, a drum- and bass-heavy collection of songs from the album of the same name.

"David was doing a drum and bass tour, which was not the most interesting performance, and came up with the genius idea that he should play Glastonbury, so invited Michael Eavis," Bowie's tour promoter John Giddings claimed. "It was at the London Astoria, and Michael walked out halfway through saying it was the most boring thing he had ever seen." The next day, Giddings lied to a journalist from the *Sunday Times*, telling them that "Glastonbury are begging David Bowie to headline – Michael was bombarded with phone calls! By the end of the day, Michael Eavis was very much, 'Oh, we always wanted Bowie!' It went quiet for about three days and we were very nervous. And then I got this message from David and it said, 'You naughty boys, don't ever do anything like that again.'"

Thankfully Bowie played Glastonbury that year, despite Giddings's ruse. And it was an absolute killer of a set. "Bowie reinvented himself, he played all of the hits and dressed up like *Hunky Dory*," continued Giddings. The week following the show, the *NME* described Bowie's festival closing gig as "Not only the greatest Glastonbury headline performance but the best headline slot at any festival ever". The show has become so iconic that it was released in all its singular glory in November 2018.

"As of 1990 I got through the rest of the 20th century without having to do a big hits show," said David Bowie in 2000. "I did four or five hits on the later shows, but I held out pretty well. I thought... big, well-known songs will litter the field at Glastonbury this year. Well, with a couple of quirks, of course."

Now helping out her father full time with the running of the festival, it was Bowie's set that made Emily remember the power of the festival. "I often get asked what the best set I've seen here at Glastonbury is, and Bowie's 2000 performance is always the one which I think of first. It was spellbinding; he had an absolutely enormous crowd transfixed. I think Bowie had a very deep relationship with Worthy Farm and he told some wonderful stories about his first time at the festival in 1971, when he stayed at the farmhouse and performed as the sun was rising. And he just played the perfect headline set. It really was a very special and emotional show."

Unfortunately, the high of Bowie's stupendous set could not last. Due to the tragic circumstances that occurred at the Roskilde festival, a week later, the year 2000 was the last time Michael Eavis could keep "the man" – the authorities – at bay. "2000 was the year all those people died at Roskilde [nine people were killed in a fatal crush during a Pearl Jam show], and the police came to me and said, 'You're not running it properly.' So I had to go to Melvin [Benn] and Vince Power at Mean Fiddler," Michael told *IQ*. There had already been some Press claiming the "event was not safe" with more than 250,000 people (125,000 of which did not have a ticket) coming to see, among many others, David Bowie. Michael Eavis had to face the truth: the festival had grown too big, too wild, and out of control. "Well, 2000 was a great festival, it was a fantastic year, I have to say," Michael told the *Guardian*. "But everyone was hopping through the fence and it was overcrowded. It was crunch time, really. So I took all that on board, and we took a year off. We designed the new super fence and I persuaded Melvin [Benn of the Mean Fiddler organization] to take on the operational mantle so that we could do the things that we do best – which is put on a show. And in 2002, Joe Strummer helped us with a campaign to encourage people to not come without a ticket and that was incredibly successful. It has been ever since, really."

With Benn onboard, Michael and his then-12 organizers could return to concentrating on making the festival the greatest show on earth.

Following a year off to sort out security in 2001, Michael had to pay fines for breaching his licence for the number of people attending in 2000. The 2000 festival saw 100,000+ people jumping the fences, doubling the numbers permitted to attend overall. Mendip District Council (MDC) refused to grant Eavis a licence for Glastonbury 2002 unless the Mean Fiddler, who have long time expertise in festival security, were brought in. In 2002, a sea of change swept through the festival management. Several weeks before the festival was due to start, security teams began erecting the £1 million, 3.65-metre (12-foot) tall "super fence".

"For years, a lot of people have been getting into Glastonbury without tickets – over or under the fence, forgery, scams, whatever," Michael told the BBC at the time. "This year things have to change for good. We are appealing to people's consciences – please don't come without a ticket. The local council have made it clear that if anybody breaks through the fence, there will be no more Glastonbury festivals."

Alongside the fence were watchtowers to stop jumpers going over and diggers going under. While the fence made the news, the truth is that Glastonbury became better because of it, and it didn't have to sacrifice its goodtime vibes in the process. If anything, the super fence kept all the love in – and kept the disappointment of the "real world" out.

With Glastonbury now perceived to be impenetrable (although inevitably the odd clever dick exposed weaknesses in the fence and was able to dig in or jump over), the 2002 festival offered a safer and altogether more controlled environment. In many ways, looking back with the benefit of hindsight, the headline band that year matched the new Glastonbury "safety first" ethos. Coldplay were the main weekend headliners. But, Coldpay were by no means the safe option at that precise time. "Coldplay, Radiohead, Oasis and lots of bands have really furthered their musical status here," Michael Eavis has said. "Certainly Coldplay, who I booked to headline on the Friday in 2002 when they weren't that well known. The agent and manager thought it was too soon but I said, 'Well, I've agreed it with Chris [Martin, the band's lead singer], and Chris wants to do it, so let's go with it'. That was a good move, it really was! Coldplay were superstars from then on."

Indeed, Coldplay's 2002 performance at Glastonbury has gone down in history as one of the best headline shows ever, despite the band playing a bunch of songs from their latest record, *A Rush of Blood to the Head*, that no one in the audience had heard yet. Phil Harvey, Coldplay's fifth member and then manager, remembers the moment of being invited to play Glastonbury as anything but safe. "Absolutely ridiculously, Michael Eavis had invited us to headline Glastonbury. We'd released one album and were still absolute minnows. For him to ask us to headline the biggest festival in the world was insane. So we knew that was the date we had to have the album out by, otherwise who would be crazy enough to play Glastonbury without even having a second album? Of course, we then missed that deadline because we

didn't finish in time, so we did end up playing Glastonbury with basically songs from the first album and half the set were songs that nobody had ever heard." Thankfully, and rather unbelievably, the band pulled it together, leaving *NME* to best sum it up: "The band's performance of 'In My Place' pushed Coldplay to a whole different level. Mournful, tender and with a plangent guitar riff so classic-sounding it seemed to have been around for a hundred years. It was like an anthem for the whole festival... bedwetters no more, they're now soul-stirring practitioners of The Big Music".

Within a year, Coldplay were one of the biggest bands in the world, allowing Michael to feel very much vindicated in his instincts. Indeed, so moved by the crowd's reaction to 'Yellow' was Chris Martin, he would tell the audience with a tear in his eye: "Best choir I ever heard in my life." Coldplay's 2002 performance, along with the safety of the fence, heralded a new era for the festival – Glastonbury 2.0. After 30 years, the festival was finally where it needed to be. Naturally, it wasn't long before Coldplay would head back to Worthy Farm. Three years in fact. The band had become world champions. "Give me mud up to my knees/The best festival in history," sang Chris Martin, adapting the lyrics of 'Politik', the opening song to the album that made Coldplay superstars.

## 2003 AND BEYOND

The carefully implemented security measures of the 2002 festival paid off. The 2003 festival has been called the "best Glastonbury to date" by at least one Eavis family member. Crime- and gatecrasher-free (sort of), more than £1 million was raised for charitable causes and the line-up was headed by Radiohead, REM and Moby – all big hitters indeed. However, it was in 2004 that punters really foamed at the mouth, when rumours began to circulate about the next possible headline act. Was it true? Had Michael and Emily Eavis really snagged a Beatle? Yes.

On the Saturday night, Paul McCartney walked out on to the Pyramid Stage and addressed almost 175,000 people. "Good evening Glastonbury – it's great to be here... finally!" And with that, the rolling hills of Glastonbury Festival came alive to the sound of the Sixties. "I'd had my eye on playing Glastonbury forever, because it's an iconic festival, and if you play music that's something you've got to look at. You think, 'Oh it would be great to do Glastonbury!'" revealed Paul before the show. "Michael Eavis said, 'Do you want to do it this year?' I said, 'Yeah, go on!' And it was great, man, really cool."

After the show, Michael told the *NME*, "Paul won the day for me. He put so much into it. He hugged and kissed me afterwards but I should have kissed him. McCartney was the strongest act by far." Paul and his band were having so much fun they overran, and were fined £1,000 by Mendip council for playing past their curfew. Michael Eavis offered to pay the fine.

2004 also saw the launch of the "Unsigned" performance competition, giving new bands without record labels the chance to perform. This was a proud moment for Emily, as that is what the festival is truly about – providing inspiration to those who see the festival as a chance of making their dreams come true. "We spend quite a lot of time trying to find the right new bands. I suppose because we champion so many new bands, and because there's so much on here, we do spend a lot of time on it. To me the exciting thing – and I love all the Pyramid, and Other, West Holts, and all the rest of it – but the stuff that I really love is just the new bands element, because it's really exciting. Especially seeing a band jump from John Peel, to Other, to Pyramid, or from Acoustic, or Avalon to Park, or whatever. You see them work their way up, like Coldplay in 1999."

## 2007: MODERN CLASSIC

Another year of mud and wet weather, but by now festival-goers had come to expect – nay demand – that craziness from Glastonbury. The 2007 festival is often regarded as having been one of the biggest and best-received years of the new millennium. It was certainly the last year in which the festival managed to retain its more or less exclusively rock and pop roots before adopting a tonal shift in direction. Primarily, this involved inviting rap artists for the first time.

2007 saw many changes to the festival's appearance and site. Firstly, everyone was given a free recycled toilet roll. Musically, the line-up was regarded as one of the most memorable ever, showcasing acts that have since gone on to become icons – in particular, the Arctic Monkeys, who played their first Glastonbury set headlining the Pyramid Stage on the Friday night. After the show, singer Alex Turner was buzzing. "It's one of the best gigs we've ever done. Ever! Just because it's... Glastonbury. It wasn't raining, and... it's Glastonbury! This is the best it gets!"

## SEE EMILY PLAY

When her mother Jean died of cancer in 1999, Emily Eavis abandoned her teaching course at university and returned to Worthy Farm to help her father with his festival. History had repeated itself, as it was at the same age that Michael lost his father and returned to the farm in order to save it. "When she died in 1999, I wanted to come home from London and support my dad – to try to fill a tiny bit of the hole she left behind," Emily told the *Guardian*. "My mum was the backbone of Glastonbury. Through the rocky days, to what it became later on, she was like the mother of the festival. She had total faith in my dad, it must have seemed like madness at times because it was chaotic and during all the traveller years because it was quite fraught. It's difficult to remember now what it was like but it was difficult at times. And being in the middle of it all, I think she had this unwavering faith and that's what made it work because it was my dad's vision and his motivation but she kept the home together and had faith in him. I don't know how many women would have stuck by their husbands as well as she did really, sticking through some really difficult times," Emily reported to CNN. "After she died, that was the first time I'd really stood back and looked at this incredible entity," says Emily. "How on earth did they do it?"

The truth is that Emily already knew how they did it. Glastonbury is in her blood. She had been living and breathing Glastonbury all of her life. It was her home. Her first memory of the festival was when she was five or six. "I can remember seeing lots of knees, people walking around, and hearing the chatter, the excitement, that energy. Seeing people through the kitchen window on their way in, looking really excited that they were going to have a brilliant time. We lived in the centre of the site. We live in a farmhouse right in the middle – there was no escape," she told *Vogue*. Growing up on the farm often meant that when June arrived, Emily would often shout from her bathroom at the travellers pitching their tents "Go back to your own garden!" But today, the baton has been well and truly handed to her, and her husband, Nick Dewey. "To be honest I have always felt a sort of responsibility for the festival. Even when I was little and I didn't have any serious responsibility, I always got that pre-festival nerves thing. It's sort of like an adrenaline rush, partly because it's our home and so people are coming onto our land, our farm. You are not just putting a gig on, it's more responsibility and that's why I have always felt that kind of responsibility, but this year in particular there is that extra pressure. I have always felt it so it's not a peculiar feeling to me, it's like here we go again," Emily told CNN.

Michael's youngest daughter, one of two children he and Jean shared, Emily Eavis is now responsible for booking and programming the line-up of the festival. "While I've got 40 years of hard work, Emily's got that fine musical vision," Michael would say. Though, naturally, Michael still signs all the cheques. "Me, my dad and my husband still sit down and discuss it all. There's so much bartering and hustle with the booking agents – you have to try and sell it. A lot of agents are not that keen on Glastonbury," Emily mentioned to the *Radio Times*.

Emily began helping out Michael in 1999, but it was in 2007 that she and Dewey became co-organizers, introducing The Park area – which includes Open air stages, late night bars and cafes, tee pee villages, art installations and an illuminated 17-metre (56-foot) Ribbon Tower that looks out over the entire festival site. The Park is the place to sit back and relax – and the Emerging Talent Competition, which is now a highly popular staple of the festival – adds even more to the site. It was Emily who was responsible for re-booting the festival in 2008 with the booking of US rapper Jay-Z... you may have heard about it?

## WHAT'S A WONDERWALL ANYWAY?

The year after Emily and her husband Nick were appointed co-organizers of the Glastonbury Festival, the winds at Worthy Farm changed direction. Again. Booking controversial headliners for the festival was nothing new – Michael had been doing it since the 1970s – but with the appointment of US rap star Jay-Z for Saturday's headline slot, it appeared the gloves were off. The Eavis family had gone too far.

With the announcement of Jay-Z's appearance, ticket sales began to stall and the festival was facing a non sell-out for the first time in decades. When the dust settled, 2008 did not produce any profits, despite being deemed a success. Part of the problem was that the media pounced all over Noel Gallagher's loudmouth quip about "I'm not having hip hop at Glastonbury. It's wrong," with many "diehard" Glastonbury fans in agreement and up in arms about a solo American hip hop mogul rapping about a life that was far removed from that of the average Glastonbury punter. "Jay-Z was actually Emily's choice," Michael told the *Oxford Student*. "That year, we were in real trouble. We weren't selling. I thought we might have to cancel, as we didn't have a headliner, but Emily said, 'Jay-Z will do it.' I said, 'Who's he?' I phoned up his agent. He was American. And he said he didn't know whether it was Jay-Z's thing. The agent said, 'we're city folk, ya know.

We're really urban and you're run by hippies from the mountains!' I don't think he really understood what we were doing at Glastonbury. So I told him that we get loads of people from London, Bristol, Liverpool, Manchester – it's all city folks. Anyway, we left it for a week and the agent came back and said he wanted to do it. In the end, it was a turning point for us," said Michael.

According to Emily, all the fuss about Jay-Z performing was about nothing. "Complaining about [bands that aren't four white males] at Glastonbury is like going to London and saying you are appalled that *Miss Saigon* is playing," she told *The Independent*. "In that case, go to *Les Misérables* instead... or the thousands of other shows. The important thing is that the headliner delivers the goods by making the crowd feel like they are part of something really spectacularly special."

The man himself, Jay-Z – usually a towering inferno of bravado – surprisingly revealed that all the commotion about his appearance affected his nerves. "It was something new for me: it was almost like we were conquering a territory. We came over and there were all these tents, it was like war! Obviously, before there was all this banter that hip hop shouldn't be here. At that point, I was like, 'Man, should I not be here? What have I gotten into?' It was one of those nervous moments right before I went on and I haven't had that feeling in a long, long time." As Michael observed after the event, "it felt like the whole culture of Glastonbury had a facelift. And it was the year before Obama was elected in America. God, it was so nicely timed, that. It's what Glastonbury does," he explained. "It's bold, it was different... and that's what Glastonbury's all about. Doing something different."

The world, and the 175,000 fans at Glastonbury that rocked up in 2008, agreed with Michael's, Emily's and Nick's decision to be "controversial". Jay-Z's performance was generally well received, opening the door for the trio to continue to push the envelope. After all, the festival was now no longer just a British concern, Jay-Z (and the furore of his invitation) had become world news, putting the festival in the minds of many international artists.

"Beyoncé couldn't wait to do it, all her friends wanted to do it," Michael said. Perhaps, out of the ashes of the entire debacle, it was Amy Winehouse who, during her now-iconic 2008 appearance, summed it up best: "Let's hear it for Jay-Z. The man has got some bollocks to come here and play the tunes you don't even know you remember. Imagine if it was some cunt like Kanye West." Kanye West performed in 2015. "I have to admit," said Michael. "I was watching the Moody Blues at the time..."

Above: The Super Fence goes up, 2002.

Opposite above, right: Bowie's return to Glastonbury in 2000: one of the best sets ever.

Opposite above, left: Paul McCartney is as loved as a solo artist as he was in his Beatles days, 2004.

Opposite below: The Pet Shop Boys had a tough job to please the all-indie crowd. They nailed it with 'Go West' becoming a campsite anthem for the rest of the weekend.

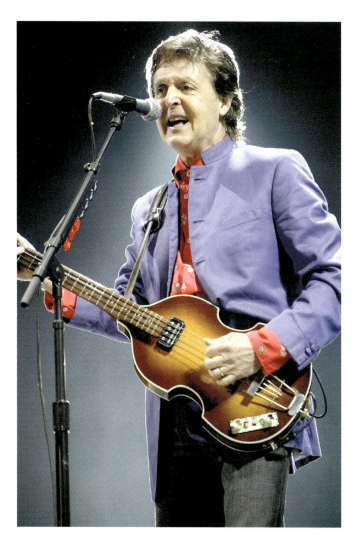

Above: The decor at Worthy Farm has always been
eclectic, 2002.

Above: Some years there's mud, some years there's glorious sunshine, 2002.

Left above: The definitive Glastonbury band – Coldplay. They've played more times than anyone else (so far). 2002. With 'In My Place' getting its first airing here, and becoming the anthem for the weekend, the band showed they had all the magic ingredients.

Left below: Gavin Rossdale, of Bush, plays in the crowd, 2002.

Opposite above: Relaxing and chilling in the healing fields, 2002.

Opposite below: "Glastonbury is tough on the cows," Michael Eavis famously told the Queen of England. "I'm a farmer first".

Overleaf: All you need is love… and a pen, 2004.

"The bands know I am not out to make money from them. How else would I get someone like Sir Paul McCartney to play for £200,000 when he might usually ask for £4 million? It's down to trust." Michael Eavis

Above: Fatboy Slim rolls out the bangers, 2003.
Below: Flaming Lips – maybe, 2003.

Below: Supergrass play an 11-song set, concluding with 'Sun Hits the Sky', 2004.

Bottom: Michael Stipe's REM headlined 2003 to much acclaim.

Above: Glastonbury festival goers bathe in a golden
sunset glow, 2003.

Opposite: Michael Eavis looks back at an old map
of the Festival site.

"The Glastonbury Festival is fun but I am a farmer first. My family have farmed the land for 150 years. I no longer get up at 5.30am every morning to milk the cows, but it is still a full-time job."

Michael Eavis

"The festival brings in about £25 million, but almost all that will be swallowed up in staging, bands, security, facilities and other costs. We only make about £2 million profit. This is shared between Oxfam, WaterAid and Greenpeace. The festival is a sell-out. We could charge more but it would spoil the atmosphere and goodwill." Michael Eavis

Above: The Black Eyed Peas, 2004.

Opposite: The Scissor Sisters are hard to miss, even when hanging out backstage, 2004.

Above: Punters preparing to enter the party, 2004.

Opposite above: Soap bubbles at dawn, 2004.

Opposite below: The sense of community at Glastonbury extends to all areas, 2004.

"In one view there is Glastonbury the fantasy land, hedonism central; but the other view is that it's also possessed by this amazing positivity, and a sense that we can change the world. Wherever else do you have that many people, in one space, that have such similar feelings and politics? No other place in the world has that."

Emily Eavis

Opposite above: Glastonbury submerged, 2005.

Opposite below: Banksy's 'Stonehenge', 2007.

Below: One of the festival's many themed areas.

Bottom left: Glastonbury mourns a broadcasting icon, and Glastonbury legend, RIP John Peel, 2005.

Bottom right: Burlesque striptease artist, Nancy, performs on stage in Glasto's newly installed "after dark naughty corner" Lost Vagueness.

Above: Amy Winehouse, shortly after the release of
her multi-award-winning album *Back to Black*, 2007.

Opposite: 2007 was a vintage year - Iggy Pop
performing on the Other Stage.

"It was a historic night for Glastonbury and for me, as it was the first time a hip hop act had headlined. But it was incredible. I'm glad it went that way, 'cause the world was watching. It felt like a moment in time. Would I do it again? Of course!"

Jay-Z

Right above: Dizzie sets faders to bonkers. 2008.

Right: Richard Ashcroft and the Verve return, 2008.

Opposite: Jay-Z performs to much controversy and acclaim, 2008. "That bloke from Oasis said I couldn't play guitar/Somebody should have told him I'm a fuckin' rock star," Jay-Z quipped at a later gig.

Above: Slash fans welcome their favourite guitarist to the Pyramid Stage, 2010.

Below: HMS Sweet Charity, a tropical discotheque, invites visitors to set sail to "dance madly on the lip of the volcano to musical alchemists and turntable Svengalis."

Top: Glastonbury goes bananas for Gorillaz, 2010.

Above: The Doggfather proved a real dogg-based treat for Glastonbury fans, 2010.

"Jay-Z changed the course of our headliners. You can't just keep repeating those old Anglo-Saxon rock 'n' roll bands. We have to move on, away from that. It changed the whole festival scene. The whole scene changed because of that decision." Michael Eavis

# DECADE PLAYLIST: 2000s

1. **COLDPLAY 'POLITIK'**
2. **REM 'EVERYBODY HURTS'**
3. **PAUL McCARTNEY 'HEY JUDE'**
4. **MUSE 'PLUG IN BABY'**
5. **BRIAN WILSON 'GOOD VIBRATIONS'**
6. **THE KILLERS 'MR BRIGHTSIDE'**
7. **JAY-Z '99 PROBLEMS'**
8. **AMY WINEHOUSE 'VALERIE'**
9. **BRUCE SPRINGSTEEN 'DANCING IN THE DARK'**
10. **BLUR 'SONG 2'**

Left above: Matt Bellamy of Muse returns to headline for the second (of three… so far) performances.

Left below: Their 2004 performance of all their sparkling gems pushed Scissor Sisters to No.1 in the UK. The glam group would return in 2010, with Kylie Minogue as a super special guest.

Opposite: Every sunset at Glastonbury is different.

2010S — NEXT GENERATION

GFRK2010/130-159

AT THE BEGINNING OF THE DECADE – GLASTONBURY'S FIFTH – THE FESTIVAL REACHED A SORT OF MIDDLE AGE, IN HUMAN TERMS. HOWEVER, INSTEAD OF BEING CREAKY, CRANKY AND FALLING APART, THE FESTIVAL WAS FIGHTING FIT: A WELL-OILED MACHINE READY FOR WHATEVER TROUBLE WAS THROWN AT IT. FOR THE NEXT DECADE, BUILDING UP TO THE FESTIVAL'S 50TH CELEBRATION BASH IN 2020, MICHAEL AND EMILY EAVIS, AS WELL AS THE OTHER KEY ORGANIZERS, PULLED OUT ALL THE STOPS. THEY CURATED AN EVEN MORE INCREDIBLE WEALTH OF PERFORMERS ACROSS THE 60 STAGES. PEOPLE CAME TO THINK, LAUGH, CRY, SING, DANCE AND MOSH...

## HAPPY BIRTHDAY

To celebrate the festival's fortieth birthday, the biggest show on earth put on the biggest show on earth. Even the sun put its hat on and came out to play, with 2010 regarded as the hottest festival ever, with temperatures rarely dipping below 27°C (80°F) during the day. Thankfully, a second million-litre water reservoir to support 800 taps around the site was installed to keep up with the heat. It wasn't just the sun who performed. Gorillaz (who replaced U2, as singer Bono was injured), Muse, Snoop Dogg, Ray Davies, Flaming Lips, Willie Nelson and more than 2,200 other diverse acts all graced Worthy Farm with their presence. It really was a vintage Glastonbury. The birthday celebrations weren't complete until Sunday night headliner Stevie Wonder closed the show with a rendition of 'Happy Birthday'. In a moment of madness, Michael Eavis was invited to sing on stage with Wonder. "When the time came they didn't give me an earplug or anything, so I didn't know what the pitch was," Michael recalled. "I can sing in tune, but I was a bit flat because I couldn't hear it!" Regardless of these excuses, Michael and Wonder singing together sent the farm into a fuzzy state of nostalgia. Orbital's Other Stage performance with Doctor Who actor Matt Smith – performing a remix of the *Doctor Who* theme – did the opposite, with revellers plunging themselves into a frenzied whirl of excitement.

The next day, at a Press conference, Michael Eavis told journalists, "It has been the best party for me – the weather, the full moon and last night a crowd of 100,000 people, every single one enjoying themselves. The best in 20 years."

After Emily Eavis's controversial decision to book US rapper Jay-Z in 2008 paid off handsomely, transforming the identity of the Glastonbury Festival into a more international event became easier. In 2011, Beyoncé – the biggest popstar in the world at the time and Jay-Z's wife – agreed to perform at the biggest show in the world. Of course, internet trolls still grumbled about her suitability for the festival, but much more quietly this time around.

Performing alongside "safe guitar bands" U2 on Friday and Coldplay on Saturday, Beyoncé provided a refreshing change of pace. While U2's set was not universally well received, with even the band claiming they "were all over the shop ... in a good way", Coldplay's set is now widely considered as one of the best ever, winning a BBC poll in 2013 as the "perfect Pyramid headline set".

The pressure was on Beyoncé, the first female headliner in 15 years, to win over a crowd that was perhaps over-stuffed on guitars. "We are really keen to keep the line-up as diverse as possible," said Emily at the time. "I went to see her live last year and was blown away by the might of the show. She has such soul, an amazing voice with an incredible, all-female band. She knows how to deliver live, and she packs a big punch – it's going to explode!" Emily told *Clash Music*. "We really want the people who are the masters of their fields, and that's what Beyoncé is. Luckily, we spoke to Beyoncé before she planned her tour this year, so she managed to put Glastonbury in her schedule, then built a European tour around it," Emily told the *Radio Times*.

As expected, Beyoncé knocked her performance out of the farm. "I still can't believe I'm performing at Glastonbury," she told more than 100,000 fans, a significant portion of the entire weekend attendance. "I always wanted to be a rock star ... this is my dream." As if to prove her rock star credentials, Beyoncé ripped into a fantastic version of Kings of Leon's 'Sex on Fire', who headlined the festival alongside Jay-Z in 2008. "Beyoncé made me masturbate to my own song," Caleb Followill, the frontman of Kings of Leon would exclaim. To be fair, it was that good.

Alongside the fun on the Pyramid Stage, 2011 also saw the founding of a new stage, the "Spirit of '71", a tribute to the festival's co-founder, Andrew Kerr. "Michael's kindly allowed me to have a stage, near the Glade stage," said Kerr. "There will be talks, and acoustic music, and things like that. I'm getting some of the old crowd [from 1971] back together." Artists such as Nik Turner, Arthur Brown, Melanie, Nick Lowe, Terry Reid and Robyn Hitchcock all performed, having remained stalwarts of Glastonbury since its inception. Andrew Kerr sadly passed away in 2014.

2011 was also the debut year of the relatively unknown and fresh-faced Ed Sheeran, who came to the site as both a punter and a performer. The singer – who had released his debut single 'The A Team' two weeks prior to the event – was one of the hottest new acts to perform, again thanks to Emily Eavis's desire to seek out such acts. "This is a massive benchmark – to play Glastonbury," the singer said.

"It's the biggest festival in Europe. You grow up and you're like, 'One day I'm going to play Glastonbury.'" Over the course of the weekend, Sheeran would perform eight times at the festival. "I wouldn't be playing eight gigs if I didn't want to play eight gigs," he later remarked. Indeed, in six short years, Sheeran worked hard and nabbed the festival's top spot by closing the show on Sunday in June 2017. "I'm actually more excited for this than I was for my Wembley Stadium shows," Sheeran told the BBC before his headline spot, "because when you're playing your own shows you're not really winning anyone over, because they've already parted with cash to buy a ticket. But I think I'm going to be playing to a lot of people who might have heard some of my songs on the radio, but they're Glastonbury-goers, they're not fans of me. Knowing that there are people in the audience who possibly don't even like my music at all and are just there to sort of see, that excites me." The singer's set was widely applauded. It was the second time just one performer had performed solo (with just an acoustic guitar and his famous loop pedal) in the headline slot, following Kanye West's solo show in 2015. "I have to admit," Sheeran told the 100,000 strong crowd, "I'm very nervous."

## A BIGGER BANG THAN EVER BEFORE

The festival returned with an even bigger bang in 2013. Before the festival, the BBC announced that this year would represent their largest broadcast coverage of the event to date, with more than 250 hours of performances broadcast on television, radio and online. It was also the first year that the BBC Glastonbury coverage went mobile, with many more than 120 gigs available to stream on computers, mobiles and tablets. Mark Friend, the director of the BBC's festival coverage said: "Not only will this be the first truly digital Glastonbury, this will also be the first mobile Glastonbury. We expect mobile and tablet viewing and listening to reach unprecedented levels, particularly over the weekend." He was right. More than 6.2 million viewers tuned in – up more than 77 per cent from 2011's festival. Bob Shennan, BBC Controller of Popular Music, said: "Glastonbury 2013 on the BBC has been outstanding. Record-breaking numbers of people tuned in to what has been our most comprehensive digital Glastonbury offering to date. This year, we gave our audience the

opportunity to watch what they wanted, when they wanted and how they wanted. And they did."

Of course, many of these viewers came for two reasons – to see Mick Jagger and Keith Richards of the Rolling Stones up on the Pyramid Stage. The BBC revealed that the band's now-iconic performance was the most requested Glastonbury programme, with more than 700,000 individual viewings.

According to Michael Eavis, in almost 50 years only three "bucket list" bands have not played the Glastonbury Festival headline slots – Led Zeppelin, Pink Floyd and the Rolling Stones. "There aren't many headliners left, we're running out!" Michael told the BBC. Pink Floyd will in all likelihood never happen, and Led Zeppelin's three surviving members have all played at the festival separately but not collectively, with Robert Plant giving his most recent performance in 2014. Perhaps Fleetwood Mac are the only other major band missing from Michael Eavis's list, but as Michael reasoned, "Mick Fleetwood said he would do it himself, but come on. I'd like the rest of the band and they all want to be paid a lot of money. We can't afford to spend £4–5 million on people to play." As Emily told the media and entertainment company Refinery29: "Glastonbury relies completely on goodwill, we're not in a situation where we're able to just give people enormous amounts of money. We probably pay ten per cent of what they would get from playing any of the other major British festivals. We're really grateful for the bands we get because when they come here they're basically doing it for fun and for the love of it."

In 2013, the Rolling Stones finally agreed to perform at the festival after being paid what Michael Eavis called "a reasonable rate." The reason the Stones finally acquiesced was, according to Michael, simple. "The Stones wanted to do it; that's the secret really. Who wouldn't want to do it? Everybody's done it except them, you see. They knew they were conspicuous by their absence."

Like Paul McCartney's 2004 set, the Rolling Stones' festival show of 2013 has now gone down in history as one of the most iconic gigs ever seen in the valley of Worthy Farm. The group's 20-song-strong setlist included renditions of stone-cold classics, as well as a few surprises thrown in for good measure, in particular erstwhile Stones' guitarist Mick Taylor playing on 'Midnight Rambler' and encore 'Satisfaction', and a choir singing on 'You Can't Always Get What You Want'. The performance was deemed by Michael Eavis to be "the high spot of 43 years of Glastonbury. They finally did it, and it was fantastic. My God, did they deliver." In stark contrast to the Stones' rock 'n'roll, it was the acoustic folk-rock of the band Mumford & Sons that closed the weekend. Last time they played, in 2008, only 200 people turned up. This year, 80,000 people were in the crowd. "We came for a party," Marcus Mumford told the thronging masses, who were all desperate for a hoedown.

2014 boasted an eclectic line-up of performers ranging from Dolly Parton in the "Glastonbury Legend" Sunday afternoon slot ("Can I get an Amen?," she hollered to the crowd!) through to the American heavy-metal outfit Metallica, who Michael had been wanting to play for two decades. This was a fact that prompted the band's singer James Hetfield to shout "Metallica. Glastonbury. Together at last!" to the crowd who, come the end of the set, were totally won over.

However, it was at the 2015 Glastonbury Festival that things got kicked up a notch with the Pyramid Stage appearance of another US rap star, Kanye West. Tickets for this weekend sold out in 26 minutes – a Glastonbury record – in stark contrast to 2008, when Jay-Z was announced as headliner. As always, rumours of potential headline acts began circulating throughout the media, a process which has become a national pastime in recent years. Fleetwood Mac, Muse, AC/DC, Prince ("We're always having a go at Prince," Michael said), Queen – all of these great names were mooted. But no one was expecting Kanye West. In fact, so unexpected was his booking that it sparked a controversy that led to a petition to ban the self-proclaimed "Yeezus" from performing. It received more than 100,000 signatures. Even betting company Paddy Power offered odds of 2/1 that West would be booed off the Pyramid Stage.

The derision hurled at Emily Eavis for her decision to book such an extreme act prompted the organizer to write an opinion editorial for the *Guardian*. "Every year when we announce who's playing at Glastonbury, there are complaints and often outrage – we're well used to that," Emily began. "Scrutiny of our headliners has become

something of a national pastime. We've had it in recent years with Jay-Z, Beyoncé, Metallica and plenty of others. We even had it in 1984 when we booked the Smiths, because people wanted Hawkwind again! This year is no different. In normal circumstances, we wouldn't add to the story by commenting. But given the enormous amount of media coverage from all corners of the globe, we felt compelled to respond this time. We think the story this year should not be: 'Why is Kanye coming?' but: 'How amazing is it that *Kanye is coming*?' One of the world's biggest superstars and a music legend, always interesting, never boring. He has agreed to play a festival where headliners get paid a fraction of their normal rate in support of Oxfam, WaterAid and Greenpeace as well as thousands of other worthy causes." Emily added that the reason people get so animated about the artists is because the festival is a victim of its own success and that criticism is inevitable because Glastonbury is such a national institution. "People feel they have ownership over it," she said. "They have an incredibly rose-tinted view of what it used to be like – whether it actually was like that I don't know."

Emily's response to Kanye West's headlining dampened the flames of ignorance, but unfortunately the "online hate" grew too much and, come the time of the gig, the pressure ultimately got the best of the performer. "I started off the show and I completely messed up the music," West told the BBC. "I'm a bit of a perfectionist, so it really put me into a slightly depressed state." The set contained a few fluffs, including a restart of the track 'Black Skinhead', following a stage invasion by "comedian" Lee Nelson, who disrupted Kanye West's flow. West also forgot the words to Queen's 'Bohemian Rhapsody', which, for those who saw the coverage, was intensely awkward. "When that music messed up in the beginning, it tapped into my nerves and when you're nervous or vulnerable, something special and something different can happen," West admitted. West ended his performance by proclaiming himself the "greatest living rock star in the world" and, judging by the rapturous ovation he received, the crowd were united in agreement. This was without doubt vindication, once again, of Emily Eavis's and her husband Nick Dewey's musical

"Headliners should be the best artists around – whether they're rappers, pop stars or rock bands. The genre is irrelevant – it's about who is going to produce the most exciting show and is making the best music. We always encounter debate, which is great, that's what it's all about."

Emily Eavis

vision. "We use our instincts. You go with who you love and who you want to have on, who's a good live act," Emily said. "We try to keep the line-up as varied as possible. That's the thing about Glastonbury – it's so diverse, not just one type of music." That said, Michael missed the show, preferring to watch the Moody Blues, allegedly telling the *NME*: "I don't do all that hip hop stuff!"

If the hiring of Kanye West was a divisive decision, Emily, Michael and the rest of the festival organizers once more came under fire in 2016 with the announcement that Adele would be performing as a headliner. Not that Adele cared. "I don't have a lot of upbeat, happy songs, which is why I think people were annoyed at me playing," she informed the BBC. "But fuck them, eh? Let's just embrace it, because I'm not going anywhere for an hour and a half."

Adele decided she wanted to perform after taking inspiration from West's performance the previous year. "I was so frightened watching his set, but said 'yeah, I'll do it'", Adele told the BBC. "I have had some of the best times of my life on a Saturday night here at Glastonbury. Moments in my life that I'll remember forever. This is, by far, the best moment of my life. I didn't want to come on and now I don't want to go off."

Adele's outstanding 15-song set was peppered not only with laugh-out-loud quotes ("Oh my God, I just burped! I had a dirty burger before I came on, that's why.") to the largest amount of swear words ever dropped on the Pyramid Stage – 33 curse words altogether. Adele's swearing was much to the annoyance of the BBC, who had pre-warned the singer about her "potty mouth". "Do you know how rock and roll I am? Not very, but the BBC had to give me a warning about my potty mouth before I went on. I bet Muse didn't get that."

Speaking of Muse – who took the top billing on the Friday night in 2016 – the band became the first ever to perform on the Pyramid Stage on a Friday, Saturday and Sunday night. "I've never enjoyed myself so much," Michael announced. 2016 also saw the return of the mud, once again causing the organizers headaches. "I've never seen mud like it in my whole life. This is worse than 1997. In all 46 years, it hasn't been as bad as this," Michael Eavis said. Nevertheless, the revellers didn't seem to care. "I drove around the whole site last night. It took right up until 4.30am and the sun was up and there was just thousands of happy people with smiles on their faces despite the adverse conditions. It is extraordinary. I do not know how they do it, but they love it so much," Michael told the *Guardian*.

The Glastonbury Festival of 2017 was an important event, with all eyes set on what would be announced next. It was the final festival before a planned year off in 2018 – in order to give the fields of Worthy Farm time in which to recover properly from the revels of previous years – and the big 2019–2020 push for the 50-year anniversary. "Wait till you see the new loos," Michael Eavis announced excitedly to the media. "No emptying – it goes straight into the ground. After 47 years, we've finally got the perfect loo!"

Yes, in 2017, Glastonbury returned with brand new toilet facilities. These were cheekily dubbed the Toilets of Dreams, and were designed to highlight the charity WaterAid's battle to ensure clean water for all those living in impoverished countries. No wonder Emily Eavis claimed the festival "... has to be the best one yet." 2017 also saw the invention of a brand new attraction, Cineramageddon, a five-day film festival within the Festival, conceived and curated by director Julien Temple. "Glastonbury is the only place in rain-soaked Brexit Britain where an outdoor post-apocalyptic drive-in cinema can possibly work," said Temple. As most die-hard Glastonbury lovers will know, he directed the 2006 Glastonbury rockumentary film, which discussed the history of the festival from 1970 to 2005. Cineramageddon screened a wide selection of classic, contemporary and popular movies and showcased talks with the director and actors, all surrounded by 70 vintage cars, repurposed funfair rides and a Learjet.

As if all that wasn't enough, 2017 welcomed something else completely new to the festival – never before experienced, a genuine first: the Foo Fighters, without doubt one of the best live festival bands in the world. Amazingly, they had never played Glastonbury before.

The Foo Fighters had been scheduled to perform at Glastonbury in 2015, but singer Dave Grohl broke his leg on stage a few weeks before and was unable to appear. Florence and the Machine were a surprising – but incredible – replacement for the American outfit.

> "I've spent years running my show and trying to curry favour with the authorities just to make it happen. I'm so pleased not only for myself, but for the hundreds and perhaps thousands of people who have had faith in me and supported my ideas through thick and thin."
>
> Michael Eavis, on his CBE, 2007

In 2017, the Foo Fighters came to the festival and thoroughly made up for their unfortunate absence two years earlier. During their astonishing 20-song set, with opener 'Times Like These' dedicated to Florence Welch, the lead singer of Florence and the Machine, the Foo Fighters did what they do best – played loud and lewd.

"We were doing an interview and someone said, 'You know you're not supposed to swear? There's no swearing at Glastonbury,'" Dave Grohl told the crowd. "And I said, 'What the fuck is that supposed to mean?' And then I guess Adele holds the record for saying the most fucks at a Glastonbury gig. I heard it was 33. Now I love, Adele, but guess what... fuck fuck fuck!" The singer went on to break Adele's record by delivering 34 fucks to the amused audience.

The Foo Fighters were not, however, the biggest stars of the weekend in 2017. That honour went to British politician and Labour party leader Jeremy Corbyn, who gave an impassioned speech to the gathered masses from the Pyramid Stage. Michael Eavis seemed generally star-struck by his appearance: "Jeremy really is the hero of the hour, and he's so refreshing. We're going to make some major changes in our society. This is the future of the country, and young people are so into it. It's bloody brilliant!"

Mr Corbyn walked out to deafening applause on the Pyramid Stage. He praised Michael and the festival. "Michael brought the spirit of music, the spirit of love, the spirit of ideas, and he brought the spirit of great messages. This festival was envisaged as being for music yes, but also for the environment, and for peace. This place in Glastonbury is truly wonderful. I remember coming to this area as a child being taken up to Glastonbury Tor by my mum and dad and thinking what a wonderful place it is, because there's something very special about it. It's a place where people come together and they achieve things."

## 50 YEARS AND 50 MORE

"Half a century. It's an incredible feat," Emily wrote in the *Glastonbury Free Press* in 2017. "We've been through so many struggles to get here." As the 50th anniversary of Glastonbury fast approaches in 2020, with no doubt the biggest Glastonbury ever planned (though obviously not announced until just before!), Michael and Emily have

begun the countdown clock to the big birthday bash. "I think I can run on another seven years, which would take me up to 50 years, then I'll see what happens after that," Michael said in 2013. With the "gradual process of Emily and Nick taking it over" (says Michael) now seemingly complete, the baton that is Glastonbury has been passed down. 2020 may see the end of Michael's time at Glastonbury, with the festival becoming one big retirement party. Or it might not. In the best Glastonbury tradition, no announcements will be made until the last possible moment. Throughout 2018, Michael and Emily announced tentative plans for a new festival, with a working title of "Variety Bazaar". "We are going to do a show somewhere else with the same team behind Glastonbury, but we're still not entirely sure what shape it's going to take," Emily told the *Guardian*. "For now we're all focused on Worthy Farm. We're not thinking too far down that road because we're quite busy with this one at the moment! It's still very much in the planning stages, but we've got to be brave enough to have a go".

It appears that once the 50th celebration is out of the way, organizers will shift their focus towards the Variety Bazaar and take the Glastonbury brand to further heights. The new festival will be, as Michael asserted to the *Guardian*, "the last big gamble in my life." Emily cleared up some confusing and mixed reports that the new festival might conflict with Worthy Farm: "We have no plans to stop doing the festival here, but we want to try something in another location away from the farm, possibly in 2021." "Worthy Farm is the home of the festival as far as I'm concerned – forever," Michael would reassert.

Opposite: Sunset view from the lounging area above the Park Stage, 2011.

Overleaf: What does 135,000 revellers look like? Aerial view of 2011's festival.

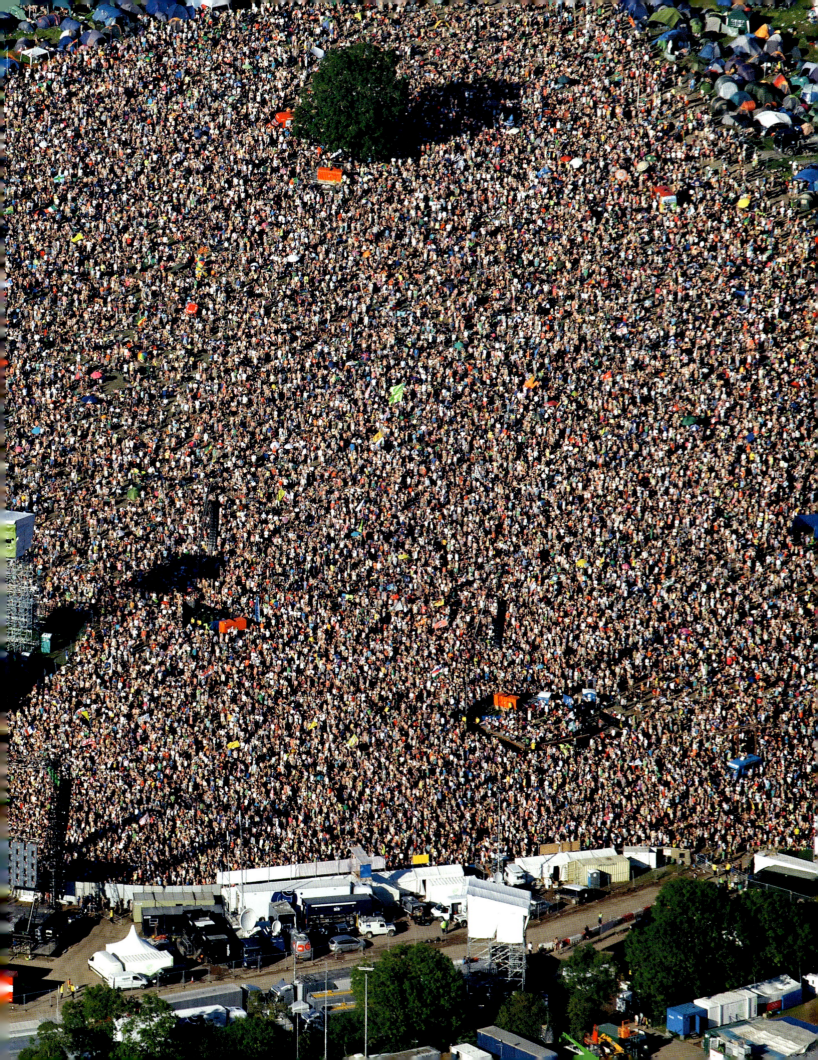

Opposite and right:
Beyoncé and U2 were
among 2011's headline
performances. Beyoncé told
the crowd "I will never forget
this" and U2, well, when
are they not great? It was a
stellar year, for sure.

Below: Performers in the newly-installed Theatre Tent show off their skills, 2013.

Bottom: Noah's Ark fancy dress? Sure, why not!

"I think the Festival brings out the best in people, and I think people really look after each other here." Emily Eavis

Top: Nile Rodgers and Chic had the night of their lives in the Legends slot, 2013. Nile would tell the world's media that playing the festival was a "turning point" in his beating his cancer diagnosis.

Right: Marcus Mumford and band Mumford & Sons enjoyed the "greatest night of their lives" during their headline set, 2013.

"So they finally asked us."

Mick Jagger, 2013

Above: Mick, Keef, Charlie and Ron finally headline Glastonbury. Fans left satisfied.

Below: Neon glowstick outfits still visible in the early light of morning, 2013.

Opposite: Soaking up the sun and the atmosphere outside the Beat Hotel Bar, 2013.

"I think the fact I love life so much is why I want to preserve it. We have to move heaven and earth now to save this planet. That's the message I'd like people to take away. But of course the main purpose for being here is to have the best time of their lives."

Michael Eavis

Right top: Banksy's 'Siren of the Lambs' food truck makes a statement, 2014.

Right middle: The famous long drop toilets and their even more famous queues, 2014.

Right: Michael's daughter Emily Eavis with husband Nick Dewey at the Festival in 2013.

Opposite: The bright lights of the Pyramid Stage beckon revellers to its hefty bosom, Saturday night, 2014.

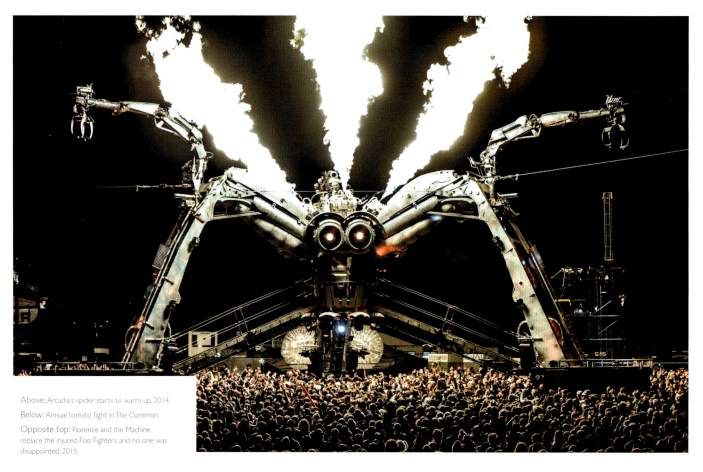

Above: Arcadia's spider starts to warm up, 2014.

Below: Annual tomato fight in The Common.

Opposite top: Florence and the Machine replace the injured Foo Fighters and no-one was disappointed, 2015.

Above middle: Kanye West proved all his critics wrong during his Saturday night headline slot.

Above bottom: the Dalai Lama's extra special appearance at the Stone Circle and on stage to address "climate issues which affect the future of mankind", 2015.

Overleaf: The festival's 46th year saw many changes. The mud stayed the same, 2016.

Opposite: Adele's 2016 performance garnered massive critical acclaim, as well as one of the largest audiences. "Fuck", she would exclaim 33 times (a then-record) despite calls from the BBC to limit her swearing.

Below: Festival flags at sunset, the day before official opening, 2017.

"For the last two days I've been spontaneously bursting into tears. I'll be really excited one minute and then I'll think it's the end of the world. I was literally expecting to come on to a soggy hay bale blowing in the wind." Adele

Above: Michael Eavis is joined on stage by Rachel Rousham, centre, from the White Ribbon Alliance as well as members of the Avalonian Choir, for a pro-feminist event organized by the White Ribbon Alliance, 2017.

Above: 2019 headliner Stormzy.
Emily Eavis describes the UK grime artist
as "perfect for Glastonbury".

Below: Ed Sheeran headlined Glastonbury 2017,
though many who watched at home were confused
by his loop pedal, claiming he wasn't playing "live".

# DECADE PLAYLIST: 2010s

1. **DOLLY PARTON** 'I WILL ALWAYS LOVE YOU'

2. **BEYONCÉ** 'SINGLE LADIES (PUT A RING ON IT)'

3. **KANYE WEST** 'FOURFIVESECONDS'

4. **ARCTIC MONKEYS** 'I BET YOU LOOK GOOD ON THE DANCEFLOOR'

5. **ROLLING STONES** '(I CAN'T GET NO) SATISFACTION'

6. **FLORENCE AND THE MACHINE** 'YOU GOT THE LOVE'

7. **DIZZEE RASCAL** 'BONKERS'

8. **FOO FIGHTERS** 'EVERLONG'

9. **ED SHEERAN** 'SHAPE OF YOU'

10. **ADELE** 'HELLO'

Left: The Foo Fighters made beautiful shapes and colours on stage, 2017.

> "Glastonbury costs £22 million to put on every year. This covers everything from the marquees to security. The festival is said to be worth £82m, £2m of which went to charity last year, including main beneficiaries Oxfam, Greenpeace and WaterAid."
>
> Michael Eavis

# CREDITS

The publishers would like to thank the following sources for their kind permission to reproduce the pictures in this book.

Key: t = top, b = bottom, c = centre, l = left & r = right

Alamy: Adam Beeson 61 c; /Guy Bell 154; /Matt Fagg 121 b; /Mike Goldwater 53-55, 88-89; /Mark Leonard 126 t; /Jamaway/Stockimo 146; /Stuart Roy Clarke 82 b, 121 t; /Edd Westmacott 86, 90 b

Courtesy of Colin Alexander: 61 b

Apex News & Pictures: Ian Sumner 48, 49 b, 50, 51, 79

Avalon: Retna/Photoshot: 62, 75 b

Bridgeman Images: PYMCA/UIG 120 t

Courtesy of Steve Bayfield: 36-40

Getty Images: Barcroft Media 153; /Andrew Benge/Redferns 11; /Bentley Archive/Popperfoto 35; /Matt Cardy 115, 116, 118 b, 120 b, 142 t, 147 t, 147 b, 156, 158-159; /David Corio/Redferns 56; /Pete Cronin/Redferns 57, 58 t; /Harry Durrant 155; /Jim Dyson 109 b, 125, 142 b, 143 t, 147 c, 149 t, 149 b; /Emulsion London Limited 150-151; /Dave Etheridge-Barnes 121 br; /Tabatha Fireman/Redferns 126b; /Jon Furniss/WireImage 98-99, 112 t; /Ian Gavan 141, 157 b; /David Goddard 138-139; /Martin Godwin 114, 118 t; /Martyn Goodacre 81 t, 84, 91 b; /Tim Hall/Redferns 42-43, 65; /Dave Hogan 127 t, 129 t, 140; /Samir Hussein 129 b, 130-131, 143 b; /Mick Hutson 4-5, 8-9, 59, 75 t, 76, 78 tl, 85 t, 90 t, 91 br, 105 tl, 112 b; /Hayley Madden/Redferns 82 t; /Leon Marks 66-67; / Eamonn McCabe/Redferns 81 b; /Vincent McEvoy/Redferns 28; /Michael Putland 80; /Brian Rasic 85 b, 119; /Rebel Media/WireImage 127; /Tony Russell/Redferns 12-13; /Nicky J. Sims/Redferns 95; /Peter Still/Redferns 83; / Jon Super/Redferns 94, 97, 106, 107, 108 t, 110-111, 113, 117; /SWNS/Photoshot 77 t;/Ian Tyas/Keystone Features 26-27, 29, 33 t; /Gary Wolstenholme/Redferns 137, 144

Mirrorpix: 22-23, 23 t, 30 t, 30 b, 31, 33 b, 34, 60, 104, 105 b, 157 t

PA Images: 23 b, 96; /Empics Entertainment 92 t; /Ben Birchall 148 t; /Matt Crossick/Empics Entertainment 144 t; /Pete Dadds/EMPICS Entertainment 74 t; / Anthony Devlin 123; /Richard Gray/Empics Entertainment 152; /Olly Hewitt/ EMPICS Entertainment 78 tr; / David Jensen/Empics Entertainment 148 b; /Toby Melville/PA Archive 108 b; /Yui Mok 122, 124, 125 b, 145 b, 149 c; /Sue Moore/ Empics Entertainment 73; /Keystone Press Agency/Zuma Press 32 l, 32 r

Gabi Pape: 34 b
Courtesy of Mervyn Rands: 24-25

REX/Shutterstock: Piers Allardyce 87 t, 91 t; /Peter Anderson/PYMCA 48 t, 52; / Duncan Bryceland 7; / /Nils Jorgensen 58, 74 b; /Hayley Madden 92 b; /Julian Mackey 105 tr; /David O'Neil/Associated Newspapers 61 t, 78 b; /Photofusion 93; /Philip Reeve 77 b; /Matthew Smith/PYMCA 64; /Stephen Seque 63; /Ray Tang 109 tr; /David White 87 b

Nick Rice: 160

Shutterstock: Steve Briscoe 128

Courtesy of David White: 19, 20, 21

Every effort has been made to acknowledge correctly and contact the source and/ or copyright holder of each picture and Carlton Books Limited apologises for any unintentional errors or omissions that will be corrected in future editions of this book.